Keepers of the Wilderness

NUMBER FIFTEEN
Environmental History Series
Dan L. Flores, General Editor

Keepers of the Wilderness

ARTURO LONGORIA

TEXAS A&M UNIVERSITY PRESS
College Station

Copyright © 2000
by Arturo Longoria
Manufactured in
the United States of America
All rights reserved
First edition

The paper used in this book
meets the minimum requirements
of the American National Standard
for Permanence of Paper for Printed
Library Materials, z39.48-1984.
Binding materials have been chosen
for durability.

Library of Congress Cataloging-in-Publication Data

Longoria, Arturo, 1948–
    Keepers of the wilderness / Arturo Longoria. — 1st ed.
       p.   cm. — (Environmental history series ; no. 15)
    Includes bibliographical references.
    ISBN 0-89096-929-9 (c) — ISBN 0-89096-942-6 (p)
  1. Natural history—Mexico—Tamaulipas. 2. Longoria,
Arturo, 1948–   I. Title. II. Series.
QH107.L675   2000
508.72'12—dc21   99-053326
                                           CIP

FOR

Sr. Ramón Longoria Gaitan

AND IN SPECIAL MEMORY OF

Sr. Abdiel González García

Contents

Before the Journey . . .	3
The First Day	4
The Second Day	11
The Third Day	17
The Fourth Day	22
The Fifth Day	26
The Sixth Day	32
The Seventh Day	39
The Eighth Day	48
The Ninth Day	55
The Tenth Day	70
The Eleventh Day	86
The Twelfth Day	95
The Months That Followed . . .	102
Works Cited	111
Index	113

Keepers of the Wilderness

Before the Journey...

All journeys, short or long, exist as mere segments of that birth to death wandering from which the lucky discern a life's purpose—its fruit the passions that wrest symmetry from chaos. This journey that is the focus of this story took place in southern Tamaulipas, Mexico, in the late spring of 1998. It is a tale of wilderness and of people, and a search to discover the roots of our behaviors toward the land. I have attempted here to present an open-minded assessment of what I encountered, specifically how culture and economic realities influence our treatment of the earth. Mexico's current socioeconomic and political climate might best be described as turbulent—the flux of increasing democratization may be upon the country, but the stresses of economic weakness and the madness of the drug trade prevail in many places. My awareness of the current political mood, and a desire to respect the privacy of certain individuals who appear within these pages, requires that I omit last names where necessary. And because I fear exploitation and development of the area visited, I have refrained from naming the river I traveled as well as the towns and ejidos (agrarian farms) of the region.

This book reflects my ideas and philosophies about nature, and I accept total responsibility for the critiques and debates that may ensue from its publication. I should note, however, that without the help of reviewers and editors, and the insights of the scholars quoted within, this work would have fallen far short of its intended mark.

The First Day

Doña María sat quietly on an old chair made from barretta wood, its ribbed back and seat and short, stout legs pegged together with dowels also fashioned from that iron-hard tree that bristled aspen white and lemon green atop the nearby hills. She was very old. Exactly how old she did not know. She said she was born sometime before the revolution. She spent her youth many miles to the south, beyond the great desert, past the cities and within a chain of mountains where an emerald jungle shrouds wet, black soil.

Earlier, as she had done every morning since she and her husband, don Miguel, first came here, she watched the sun drip skyward like a drop of yellow sap bubbling from the smooth limbs of the tall limoncillo trees that sprouted stoically from the jagged ravines and dark canyons.

With one eye an opaque white, the other a violet blue, she sat quietly thumbing and touching, as if it were a Braille known only to her, the little pile of black beans in her aproned lap. Her small, dark hands—a mosaic of creases and pleats—worked slowly and methodically, coursing over the smooth seeds, searching for the chatter, that rocky babble, that was quickly eliminated onto the ground.

"Tienes niños?" I asked, sitting lazily to her left on an aluminum folding chair I'd grabbed from the Nissan pickup's bed.

She mumbled something quickly. And I strained to understand her frail voice, the sound of tiny wooden flutes blown in random discord.

"Did you say, 'three children'?" I asked.

She nodded her gray head, her aquiline nose, bony and brown and wrinkled like her hands, bobbing conspicuously.

"Do they live nearby?"

"No," she mumbled, shifting a dark green rebozo across her short and terribly hunched back. "Mi hijo, el más grande, vive en Monterrey. Y tengo una hija. Vive en Matamoros."

I waited nearly a minute, but she said nothing more.

"I understood you to say three. What of the third child?" I finally asked.

An uncomfortably quiet moment followed. Doña María's fingers still roaming the beans, her sightless lens searching her mind perhaps for words yet to be spoken, her living eye glancing restlessly at a brown chicken pecking manically at the dirt nearby.

At last, the silence was broken. "No sé donde está mi otro hijo," she said apologetically. "Estaba en la cárcel. Pero me dijieron que possiblemente se murió unos años pasados."

"You don't know if he is alive or dead?" I asked in disbelief and wondering what prison he was in or had been in.

She shook her head, her fingers moving precariously over the beans.

To the east and southwest settled a haze nearly as opaque as doña María's blind eye: that polluted waste of modern humans, a thief of vision and spoiler of the soul.

I looked straight up. The sun had moved beyond the morning's midline. Two black vultures, wings lying flat against the wind, sailed lethargically northwest following breezes from the great Gulf of Mexico.

This is a place of transition. A land in between, of mixtures of people and plants and animals. I stood now at the northern edge of the limoncillo forests and at the southern boundary of *el monte tamaulipeco*—the Brushlands of northern Mexico and South Texas. I'd journeyed from my home in Texas across the Río Grande and through terrain that in my youth sprawled outward and into the horizon a vast spectrum of mesquite, ebony, palo blanco, nopal, and over a thousand other Brushland plants, their colors and shapes a cumulous fusion of diverse living forms. Now all of that has been replaced by fields that in drought become deserts. For as far as the eye can see.

My journey began on paved roads that gradually became more potholes than asphalt. What followed were flat caliche beds that fizzled into a consortium of gravel and clay, and ultimately atop sediments of limestone stacked hundreds of feet high.

I looked to the south. Within fifty kilometers of this spot the land changes even more. The cerros merge into mountains, the language becomes an even richer mixture of Spanish and Indian, the birds are substantially more tropical, the trees larger and higher.

Doña María stood, the beans wrapped carefully in her apron. She walked bent and stiffly to her small *jacale*—a kitchen hut and a bedroom hut separated by a narrow porch laced overhead with thickly matted grass the golden color of wheat fields ready for harvest. I stood as well, and moved into the shade of a large tree that looked like a mesquite, the same knurly bark, only blacker, with minute, bipinnately compounded leaves. But it was not a mesquite. Doña María had called it simply *la piel negra*.

We had arrived the previous day, Juan and I. An hour before nightfall, a coppery sun wedged between distant charcoal clouds with long streams of orange and pink light spreading outward from their epicenter like an enormous hand fan. It had taken us the greater part of the day to reach that summit—the lip of a long escarpment, actually.

But on the first morning only sparse clouds sailed north by northwest. Below, the river ran as swollen and brown as a great manatee, plodding its waters southward then turning abruptly to the west, like a flipping tail, at the mountain where I intended to spend a few days alone.

They call the mountain—that far-off slumberous green mound with two great white limestone rocks etching thin, sorrowful eyes on its north face, and an outcropping of suspended granite drooping noselike in between—La Viuda. Indeed, if you let your imagination carry you, she looks, as the name implies, like an old and sad widow. Like doña María, maybe. Though don Miguel was at the time still very much alive.

People say La Viuda cries for the ones who lived on and around her long ago. Earth People—*la gente de la tierra*—the locals call them in legends and songs. I was told that as I approached her, I would see tears streaming from the inside corner of her right eye. Black tears washing downward over green rock skin and into the languid river below.

She is reachable only by boat. So I had brought a fiberglass canoe, seventeen feet long, cobalt blue. Juan towed his aluminum jon boat, fourteen feet of olive drab.

Don Miguel and Juan had driven the Nissan pickup into town to buy canned goods and fruits and vegetables. I planned to take half of the food with me to the mountain. Juan, with the rest of the food, would remain at don Miguel and doña María's ranchito.

I sat alone in the shade watching a flock of yellow-headed parrots screeching hysterically as they passed the canyon that plunged but a few feet to the west of my perch. From deep inside the canyon's shadows came the whistle calls of rufescent tinamous. At my left, down the thorny slope that joined the big river, several crows cawed hoarsely.

I looked to the southeast. Far in the distance—only a pale tan speck without binoculars—lay a long strip of barren, windswept land. When I had asked don Miguel about it earlier that morning, he had said the place—"el desierto"—was all that remained of the agrarian farmers who had been herded in by the Mexican government a decade past. Part of a great dispersal from the crowded cities, the "farmers" were told to "make the land productive." The government, as don Miguel described it, escorted the agrarians in behind giant bulldozers. The land was stripped, not clean but naked. Soon the soil—but a few inches of organic matter covering endless slabs of limestone rock—blew away, to be replaced with glassy sand as lifeless and unproductive as the bleaching bones of a few cows and horses abandoned to starve after the agrarians left. Or escaped. Back to the cities of Mexico and to the United States, to huddle in boxes—brick, block and wood—and defecate at one another's sides and smell the smells of development and decay.

"Esa gente nada más querían robar de la tierra," don Miguel had said earlier, sipping his morning coffee and scratching sparse, white whiskers on his sun-darkened face.

The land owned other scars as well. To the south, beyond the great widowed mountain, logging was under way. Both Juan and don Miguel had told me that a large group of workers, directed by a man whose ownership of the land was spurious, had begun to clear-cut the forest.

"No dejan nada," don Miguel had said.

"It's true," Juan had added. "They're cutting everything down. For firewood. For fence posts. To make charcoal. Leaving nothing but piles of brown leaves and a few sticks here and there."

I felt old and tired. From those who sit steeped in their egocentric opiates to the lords of industry and commerce who preach endlessly the sermons of economic development—*Let us grow until we pop!*—I wanted no more.

To the mountain, I looked. If she was a widow, then I was an orphan.

"I'm going to go walking," I said to doña María. The sounds of frail flutes emerged from her mouth, but I did not understand what she said. She waved. That was good enough.

I lifted my walking stick from the small trailer that held the canoe and jon boat and a large metal box full of camping gear, and I began walking slowly down the wagon path that led up the hill to the ranchito. From under the three inches of my cotton hat's brim I swallowed intensively the world around me. Observing the trees and shrubs, and the birds that lit and sang within them, I listened also to the sounds flowing out from the forest. Hollow sounds, shrill sounds, thumping sounds, cackling sounds, whistling sounds, cooing sounds, barking sounds, pecking sounds. Maybe I wasn't so old after all.

I sat on a large white boulder, not old perhaps, but lonely. *The writer's curse?* I wondered. Never quite able to leap off that solitary ledge into the world's fluids and milieus; the writer sits and watches and thinks and remains alone.

A gray fox appeared suddenly. It crossed the path less than twenty yards away. It never saw me, but materialized as if extruded spontaneously from the large-leafed plants lining the trail, only to be reabsorbed on the other side within a solid mesh of green.

Wow, I thought.

I stood and walked to the place where the fox had crossed. It may have been standing just a few feet away. But the understory of herbaceous and woody plants was so thick and entwined that I could not see even four feet into it. I walked on. *Slowly.* Down the path, around a gentle curve to the right, down farther, a curve to the left, along a level stretch, until I came to a corpulent log lying parallel to the narrow wagon road. I noted that the Brushland trees that reached their terminus in this region were many times larger than what I was accustomed to in South Texas. I had passed a palo verde with branches webbing frenetically outward, its limbs dragging the ground and then swooping upward like huge serpents. There had been a stand of brasils, each at least thirty feet high. Along a cliff edging a canyon I'd admired a line of about twenty giant ébanos, the lot of them torquing skyward like Athenian gods overlooking their domain. But there were also many plants and trees that I had never seen before. There was a time when I would have carried field guides and I would have worked my way steadfastly through the keys, trying to identify each plant. I still do that sometimes, but I must admit that breaking nature down into as many objects was not what endeared me to el monte verde in the beginning. Instead it was the total experience—that rush of emotions that was the summation of the whole, indeed the very subjectivity of the encounter—that formed and nurtured my passion for the earth.

A deliciously cool breeze was gushing up the hill, gaining strength as it flowed unmolested along the trail. I closed my eyes and breathed deeply. And I thought about the mountain, and what it was going to be like to be there alone.

A sound carried through the air. Immediately, I recognized it: Juan and don Miguel were returning.

The night had come. The day had turned hot and muggy. But now it was cooling rapidly. We sat in a tight circle around a small fire. Doña María was sitting, once again, on the barretta chair. I was back on my folding chair. Juan was sitting on his homemade canvas cot. Don Miguel sat next to doña María on a flat stump of some large tree.

We had a visitor. He had returned with Juan and don Miguel. His name was Pablo. He was thirty or thereabouts. He was sinewy with well-defined arms and short athletic legs. He wore a pair of cut-off white jeans and a tattered black T-shirt with the San Antonio Spurs logo on the front. His feet were wrapped in leather thongs secured tightly to tire-tread huaraches. His skin was as red as burnt umber, his eyes dark—his hair long and straight and black as night. He laughed a lot, and sang songs and played his Mexican guitar. And so did I.

Music—a language more complex than any mathematics. No, it is not mathematics. It does not have to be reduced to signs and symbols in order to be enjoyed, or even understood. It transcends all vocabularies. It speaks directly to the soul. And yet, it has as many words as all the spoken languages the earth has ever produced, if only you try to understand it. Those, I think, who can do it well are greater than Einstein or Newton or Galileo. Of course, we did not do it well. But we didn't care. We played chords and sang songs, and taught each other new ways of looking at the world without explaining it.

Juan stood to dance. Without his hat, his bald, sweating head mirrored the fire's light. He twisted when we played "La Bamba." He held an imaginary partner when we played a polka. But when I played one of my songs, with Pablo trying to follow the inverted and augmented chords that speak to me, he watched and listened.

"Bravo," Juan said when I finished. "When did you write that one?"

"The other night," I told him. "It came to me in a dream, though I was awake at the time."

"Play it again," he said. So I did:

>When the night whispers in the wind
>And I feel the pillow on my head
>And I see the oceans sweeping over time
>I can hear the memories of you
>
>Golden sun and far away wooded cloud
>Will you wait to find me in the rain
>Will you see the lonely bird flying in the sky
>Will you hear the call of the wild
>
>Silent trails on blanket leaves of brown
>Can it take an old friend away
>Can it sigh a spirit calling from within
>Under stars and milky way
>
>When the day christens a new sun
>I will not begrudge at all
>If the mists of morning bring flowers birds and breeze
>It is all I'll ever need.

The Second Day

It sprinkled during the night. Not much, but enough to make the morning damp. A line of dark clouds hung heavily in the air. I was slow to awake, but doña María and don Miguel were up before dawn, as were Juan and Pablo. When I exited the tent I could not see La Viuda; she was shrouded by the morning mists. I had not slept much. The anticipation of today, the foreignness of my surroundings contributed to my insomnia. So I was anxious to be off. I would sleep when I arrived at the mountain. *Alone.* I needed to be alone, and I hated feeling lonely.

We had sung and talked until midnight, Juan and I, and Pablo. Don Miguel and doña María excused themselves around ten. But the three of us continued talking about this place; this was Juan's fourth visit to the area. Though he had never been to the mountain, he had boated by it on two occasions. He was the one who told me about the Earth People. Pablo had heard the stories as well: They had lived in huts made of rocks and wood. They were very shy. They were fishermen and hunters. They existed secretively. Who discovered them, and exactly when, was not known.

Word began to filter into the settled areas that a mysterious people lived on and around the mountain with the old woman's face. Then suddenly they disappeared. *Vanished.* And the stories and songs emerged. "La Viuda está llorando . . ."

"But why a widow?" I asked.

Pablo tugged at his ear, hidden behind long straight black hair. And shrugged. "Una viuda. Sin esposo. Y sin hijos."

"I can understand not having any children—if the Earth People were hers and she lost them. But who was her husband?" I persisted.

Juan was watching the fire, his angular profile and high forehead and thick eyebrows and full red beard looking so damned European and out of place. "Maybe there was an Earth Father," he mumbled.

He must have caught the face I made, because he turned to look at me, hazel eyes alive in the firelight. "You know, the mother gave them their home, the father gave them their life."

"You mean their culture their father?" I said.

Juan nodded, raising his eyebrows and dropping the corners of his mouth.

"My grandfather met some of them," Pablo said.

"What did he say about them?" Juan asked, surprised.

"He said they were small and dark. The men wore a long leather cloth around their waist. The women wore leather—a very white leather—around their chests and hips. He said their shoes were made from rabbit skin and leaves." Pablo laughed. "But my grandfather was always drunk. Nobody believed him."

"So who actually saw them?" I asked.

Juan smiled. "I can't find anybody who has ever known anyone who saw them." He paused. "Until now, that is." And chuckled. "Sometimes I think it's just a damn legend. You know, like the leprechauns."

"They were there," Pablo reasserted.

Both Juan and I could tell that Pablo would not consider it polite to challenge him, or to persist further in wanting details and evidence. So we talked about it no more.

Instead, we discussed Juan's role in all of this. He wanted to look at the stars. His mountains are light-years away. Or perhaps they, like the Earth People, are there no more. We now perceive only remnants of the glory that was. So when he is not working as a mechanical engineer he comes to this place. When there is no moon, with his big and clumsy reflector telescope, which he sets up in front of don Miguel and doña María's jacale to study the heavens. Which, out of politeness, he did not do that first night in camp, though he wanted to.

I could smell doña María's coffee as I walked out of my tent on the second morning. Pablo and don Miguel, nearly as hunched over as his wife, were sitting under the little porch between the kitchen hut and the bedroom hut. They stopped talking and looked at me as I approached.

"Buenos días," I said.

"Buenas," said don Miguel.

"You will be off in the boat today?" Pablo asked.

"Yes."

"It will be good today," said don Miguel. "If it stays cool."

"Yes," I agreed.

"Algo huele bien rico." It was Juan walking up the goat path that led from the jacale down to the river. He yawned. "You are up, I see."

And I was immediately embarrassed. Because I had slept the latest, though the sun was barely halfway above the horizon.

"We'll eat and then I'll be off," I said, wanting to be away from people.

"Better let it clear up some, don't you think?" Juan said.

"It will clear soon," said don Miguel.

Doña María was busy in the kitchen hut. When I peeked inside she mumbled something, but again the frail flutes eluded me. She walked out carrying a wooden platter with four plain clay bowls, each filled with black beans. She gave each of us a bowl, then stepped back into the kitchen hut, only to reappear, the platter this time laden with hot corn tortillas. Juan had opened three cans of sliced peaches. And don Miguel had cut four avocados that Juan had bought in town yesterday.

We ate quietly, the dark clouds churning just a stone's throw above us, it seemed. But it did not rain again. An hour later, I was ready to leave.

When I shoved off, I felt the fiberglass canoe ponderous and slow. Juan and I had attached crossbeams to the craft, each beam dangling an aluminum float at its end, thus increasing the boat's load-bearing capacity. On seven narrow wooden strips that held the crossbeams in place, we fashioned a stretched canvas deck. Stacked with boxes of food and a special umbrella sail that Juan had built—and fishing gear, tent, medical kit, water purifier, Dutch oven, and extra clothes—the pontooned canoe trudged across the water like a stick pushed through petroleum grease.

The clouds were dissolving. Two black cormorants darted out from behind a small inlet to my right and raced but inches above the water toward the limbs of a dead tree a hundred yards away. I had not intended to take a gun with me, but Juan's logic prevailed.

"Look, take this twelve gauge single shot. You're going to be out there completely alone. For at least a week. The gun will serve double duty. These shotgun shells here are signal flares. If you run into trouble, then you can fire a flare. I'll aim my telescope at the mountain every evening at eight o'clock. I'll be able to see a flare easily with the scope. And these shells in this box are double-ought buckshot—just in case you run into something."

At my side, wrapped in plastic, was the break-open twelve gauge. Besides this, Juan had a .30-30 carbine with him, an old and battered rifle he left with don Miguel. El viejito kept the Winchester in a large wooden box in the bedroom hut. Juan said he had invited don Miguel to use the rifle if he wanted to, the only request being that he oil it lightly afterward. But the old man never touched it: "Esos trienta-trientas dan una patada bruta. No, olvídate."

Pablo and Juan pushed my canoe into the deeper water as I steered the heavy craft into the river's current. Doña María had fixed me a "lonche" of scrambled eggs and potatoes with red chile tucked inside thick tortillas de harina. I placed each of the five tacos in its own aluminum wrap and stored them in a waterproof bag.

The big river's current soon caught the canoe, and using my paddle as a rudder, I drifted laggardly, the mountain directly ahead revealed suddenly from beyond the clouds.

I looked back and waved.

"Mucho cuidado," Juan yelled.

I nodded and turned to watch the mountain.

An hour passed, then another. But I had coasted only a few kilometers. I glanced at my pocket watch, then reappraised my distance from the mountain. At this pace I would be lucky to reach her by nightfall.

I perused the fiberglass canoe, noting the knotted heavy nylon rope firmly holding the aluminum pontoons, making sure the thinner nylon cord that entwined the boxes and gear was taut, seeing that my guitar, which was in its case and wrapped in plastic, was dry. Everything looked okay. Not much to do but sit, steer, and wait. The mountain would come to me soon enough, and I to it.

To my left, along the river's edge, soft-shelled turtles—their backs a muddy olive green—held tenaciously to the edges of morose limbs long dead and protruding ghostlike from the water. Their necks craned, their heads jutting skyward, the turtles eyed me with a detached curiosity. Occasionally, one would drop into the water, the splash but a dull *plop* across the expansive river.

Another hour passed. The mountain was still far away, though it seemed close. With nothing to do, I had eaten three of doña María's tacos. And I had drunk almost a quart of water. I was growing uncomfortable.

It was not a good idea to try to steer this cumbersome craft toward the shore. But the thought of doing anything here, in the middle of the river, seemed—to this reclusive being—unthinkable. What if someone was watching from the shoreline? Besides, my personal water ethic would not allow it. I, too, would drink from this somnolent stream when I made camp.

To the shore. In haste.

The canoe bumped solidly against the narrow bank under an overhang of tall trees dispersing wide shadows over sleeping water. Quickly, I moved forward, tied the canoe to a big rock, grabbed a small shovel, then headed inland through spiraling vines and wet-barked trunks. My business completed, I walked, relieved, back to the boat.

Now my problem was to reclaim the deeper water. I waded into the river and carefully began turning the canoe around. On board again, I labored to move back into the river's mainstream. It took a full twenty minutes before I was back on course, the exertion having drained most of the quart of water I had drunk beforehand. Soaked with sweat and cooking in the midday heat, I removed my shirt and replaced it with another.

An hour later the afternoon clouds coalesced, their bellies blackening. I worried about rain and even more about lightning. But I saw neither. The clouds, nonetheless, masked the haze I had first seen that morning.

By late afternoon it was obvious that I would not reach the mountain in one day. So I turned the paddle-rudder at a hard angle and pointed the canoe slowly to port and to the green shoreline. I tied the boat to the sloping branch of a tree partially immersed in the water and began preparing a place on the canoe to sleep. Twenty minutes later nightfall swept in with a sudden brush of blackness.

As I sat cocooned in mosquito netting, I looked up at endless stars. I have seen starry nights in the mountains of New Mexico, Colorado and Montana. I have slept under the stars in Michigan's Upper Peninsula. I have lived in the South Texas Brushlands and seen the stars there. But none of those places compares to what I witnessed that night.

Had it not been for the cramped confines of my mosquito hut, the thin netting propped up by two paddles wedged tightly between cardboard boxes, I think I could have stood and plucked easily one of those stars—ruby, diamond, blue sapphire—and held it gingerly, the glowing brilliance as light as a parrot's feather and as magical as a fairy tale.

I thought about Juan. He was probably already in those stars, dancing his merry, bearded head against the bosoms of nebulas and galaxies. I thought about my children, two grown and gone, two still at home. I thought about my wife. I thought about all life past, like those distant constellations unreachable. I watched, wishing I could sleep, but knowing sleep would not come easily until I reached the mountain.

I leaned forward and touched the warm receiver of the twelve gauge shotgun, a double-ought round nudged coldly inside its chamber. Then I listened. On the shore, not far from where my tethered craft drifted, an owl hooted. And some kind of night bird whistled in melancholy monotones. I heard a fish jump a few yards away. And I saw the shadows of shadows, those ultra black holes into which light vanishes, and from which the imagination pulls forth goblins and witches. I drew the twelve gauge closer to my side.

Sometime after midnight (I had managed somehow to release the mental tether keeping me awake) a hard jolt rocked the canoe. Startled, I awoke shotgun in hand. The boat bobbed, rippling aftershocks treading their way from bow to stern. I reached for my flashlight, and through the netting I scanned the water, brown and turbid.

Nothing.

I turned the flashlight off and listened. A bird, the same one or one of its kin, still whistled in melancholy monotones back in the woods.

Had it been a giant gar? Or perhaps—my pulse quickened—an alligator? I knew that alligators lived in some of the Mexican rivers to the north. But I wasn't sure if they were found here. An alligator might even try to work its way onto the boat. It would grab me by a leg. I'd awake to the searing pain at my ankle and calf . . . *my last breaths gulping water mixed with silt and algae.*

The Third Day

I awoke to a cacophony of shrieks, calls, and whistles that fell upon me from within a thicket of fluttering leaves. Dark green, yellow green, olive green leaves, draping shrubs and trees that crowded fervidly against the water's edge. I stretched and looked out across the river. A thin mist rose somnolently from the water's surface, the warm air above it as still as a picture. My back was a bit cramped, so I stood and stretched again, then grabbed my binoculars and turned to look behind me.

The sun had yet to reveal itself above the small mountains the Mexicans call cerros, though I could see by the light casting over the peaks that the day was already well under way. I scanned the trees, trying to glimpse the birds that were the cause of the ruckus. The wrap of foliage was intense, but I spotted a streaked flycatcher winging between two small trees. (At first I thought it was a sulfur-bellied flycatcher, until it landed and I saw plainly the yellow eye stripe and pale chest.) Then on the thin limb of a legume, I spotted a male barred antshrike—the sight of which almost caused me to fall out of the canoe.

I watched the antshrike, the avian counterpart to the zebra, for as long as it let me, a couple of minutes at least. It is not a particularly rare bird; nonetheless, the way the black and white feathered lines produce a stark contrast to a backdrop of greens and browns, and the way its giggling hiccup call resonates comically through the woods paints in subtle, almost imperceptible tones, a contrasting glimpse of nature, an embellishment that broadens the overall experience.

It was time to eat and be off. I opened a can of mixed fruit, ate the works, then drank the syrup. One last pan of the binoculars against the trees and onto the cerro behind me, which the sun had still not breached. I placed the binoculars in my daypack, stepped out of the canoe, and untied the nylon rope. Back in the canoe I began paddling with deep strokes into the river's mainstream.

Twenty minutes later I was pointed straight at the mountain. Behind me lay distant blue hills, that long escarpment on which don Miguel and doña María lived, and where Juan was probably sitting with the old folks under the thatched porch of their jacale: drinking his morning coffee, eating black beans and corn tortillas, with an avocado and some peaches thrown in for good measure. Knowing Juan, he'd aim his telescope at the river today to see if I was still on it. He'd better hurry, because in a couple of hours I'd be lodged on the sands that the great river has deposited at the base of La Viuda before it winds westward and south and west again and then east and onward.

A school of fish bubbled the water's surface. I became so intent on watching them that I didn't notice the approaching sound of the airplane that appeared suddenly, like a cruise missile, a flash of white and red streaking but a few feet overhead, the feculent fumes from its twin engines a garrote drawn tightly around me. I yelped and ducked and coughed, and watched the plane hug the river until it was over land, its wings tilting left and right as it worked its way within a few feet of the treetops between two large hills. A second later, it was gone—heading north by northwest and toward the Texas border.

The plane was undoubtedly smuggling drugs. I recalled the days when I was an investigative reporter, and a DEA agent asked if I knew anything about a man who owned an immense ranch located about fifty kilometers from this area. I told him I had heard the name he gave me, but that was all. He said the man was considered one of the top drug lords in the state of Tamaulipas. The man, he said, controlled the flow of marijuana and cocaine along a strict corridor that emptied into Hidalgo County, Texas. Later I heard that the man—*el mafioso mero mero de esta area*—had fled to Europe after another drug lord employed the Mexican federal police to chase him out.

Unfortunately, that is how it has become here, thanks to the ever present demand for drugs in the United States. There are many drug lords, each with his own corridor (think of it as a franchise of sorts) funneling narcotics into Texas. There are multifold methods of transport. The old, and still viable, way is to "mule" it across the Río Grande in a small boat. And every day tons of drugs cross right under the noses of U.S. Customs inspectors at the various ports of entry—despite sniffer dogs and high-tech (and high-priced) snooping equipment.

But the airplane has become the best mode of transport; some would say that despite assorted risks, it is the safest method as well. The airplane that had just whizzed over me would continue shadowing the land, taking a well-thought-out trail, keeping to the hills then over what wooded places remained until it reached the Río Grande. From there it would be but a few more miles to its drop-off point. The plane would either land, the narcotics being pushed out of a door as it turned around to take off, or it would circle low to the ground and drop the drugs to a crew waiting below. The money the pilots get for such heroics is substantial, the adrenaline rush singular, the chance of an accident unquestionable.

A Texas state narcotics agent asked me once if I wanted to fly with him and a pilot turned "confidential informant" from an airstrip in Hidalgo County to a clandestine landing field in southern Tamaulipas.

"We'll be flying at about forty feet off the ground, going over two hundred miles an hour," the narc said.

"Sounds interesting," I replied.

"Wanna go?"

"Well, yeah. When will we be leaving?"

"Tomorrow, at about one in the afternoon."

And on that day when I was supposed to fly into Mexico in a souped-up, twin-engined plane, my son Matthew was born. I'm glad, now that I've had time to ponder such foolishness, that I was at the hospital calling my friend the narc to say I wouldn't be able to make the trip.

"Oh well," he said. "We'll be going again in a week or two. You can go with us then."

But I never did.

The quiet returned. I was surprised how quickly the episode with the airplane was pushed out of the total experience. The mountain was getting closer. A belted kingfisher was darting back and forth along the river's edge, skimming the water then climbing rapidly and banking sharply like an F-16 fighter performing for the crowd at an air show. Well, perhaps the thought of airplanes hadn't completely left me.

When I neared the mountain I looked up and up and a strange fear came upon me. The clouds that passed overhead made La Viuda seem as if she was falling. I tried not to look at the summit, now less a face than a juggernaut against the clouds of black, white, and gray. Instead, I kept my eyes on the mountain's base, fixed on the wide sandy bank, trying not to look up. But like the child who cannot resist the temptation, I kept glancing skyward.

Look at it! Look at it, you fool. It's an illusion. It's not falling. It's there, and you are here. *Deal with your fears or they will own you.*

The canoe slid onto the sandy bank with more force than I would have expected. I jumped out, looked up at the mountain, laughed foolishly, stretched my back, grabbed the heavy nylon rope, and dragged the boat as far onto the sand as I could. It was a bit after one o'clock. The sun had reached its apogee and begun its fall into the western sky. I took a few more steps and realized I was feeling dizzy, perhaps from exposure on the river, and my muscles ached from the paddling and long hours sitting.

I tied the craft securely to a tree growing beyond the narrow beach, at a wall of trees that crowded the sand and blocked off the sun, and like an earth worked palisade stood guard over a forest that climbed steeply upward, toward those monstrous white eyes of exposed limestone and into that immense nose of granite rock, then upward and on, seeking the clouds, into heaven itself, where at the mountain's peak the trees stood like distant microbial specks.

Where shall I set my tent? . . .

Don Miguel had said it would be safe to camp on the little sandy beach. The river, he said, was not prone to rising suddenly, but instead maintained a rather constant level. Nonetheless, I considered establishing camp on a long, flat table that pushed out at the base of the mountain about fifty yards from the shore. But I abandoned the idea. It would mean hauling all my gear, over several trips, inland and then upward by about one hundred feet.

"I'll stay here," I mumbled. On the sand, though not right by the water.

I set my green nylon dome tent under the trees, cooled by the shade and the moist air currents flowing unceasingly atop the great river.

I built a small campfire then sat watching its smoke—that metaphysical proclamation of union with earth and universe. In my life I have known other places that were like this: pristine and alive. So many of them though are no more. Why they were destroyed and what it is about us that enables us to desecrate the earth, seemingly without remorse or anguish, has perplexed me. Is it a skewed logic permeating our culture? Or is it a characteristic innate to the human condition? As of late, we ask ourselves about the quality of our lives, and when we attempt an answer we issue forth numbers and graphs and go about counting the things we have. Quality has become quantity. And all things are considered objects simply for our pleasure.

A man could spend a lifetime here and never really know it, I thought. And still I wondered, how would the economist, the scientist, or the business person gauge the quality of this place?

I was tired and achy, and for now those thoughts would have to wait. I spent the remaining afternoon resting and bird watching, and listening to the sounds around me, and wishing that all my life could be spent like this. And perhaps as well, wishing that one would never have to argue or struggle to keep nature uncontrived.

The Fourth Day

I brewed my coffee in the light of a sun yet to appear. I was well rested, having gone to bed within an hour after sunset. The night had been quiet and exceedingly dark under those tall trees. I'd kept the shotgun close to me, not because I was afraid of the animals but just in case there might be people about. Don Miguel and Juan had warned me to watch out for men who might be hiding in the deep woods.

Hiding from what? I'd asked.

From los judiciales y los soldados, they said.

I fixed a cup of oatmeal in boiling water, sipped my coffee, and watched the morning ripen before me. Earlier, at the first breath of light, I had walked to the river's edge and cast a muted line into somber waters. The hooked, silver spoon sank for a second or two, followed by the gentle wheeze of a slowly turning reel. Within a few minutes I'd caught a black bass. That was enough. I cut the fish into fillets then placed them on a grill braced on rocks holding between them a small heap of pulsating coals. I listened to birds' sunrise cackles and calls. There was a quality in the morning, perhaps because there were no numbers attached to it.

After purifying some water (there was a time when this would not have been necessary, but agricultural chemical pollution upriver now forces one to take such precautions), I set out to explore the base of the mountain. For no particular reason I decided to walk west along the beach. Within a hundred yards, however, the bar of sand melded into the limestone bedrock that made up the mountain proper. I noticed a narrow ravine—twisted roots braiding back and forth within it. I bent low and walked into it. Almost immediately the ravine began to climb, the trees and shrubs lining it darkening the ascent but for a few isolated spots where daylight diffused brightly onto ground curdled by the mud that had last surged through it, now hard as rock.

Using the roots as steps and handholds, I moved upward, sweating profusely, my heartbeat accelerating as the angle of ascent grew more acute. I must have climbed about three hundred feet before the ravine became so steep that it was impossible to go farther. I looked down, realizing that a slip could be serious. Carefully, I backtracked, making sure my footing was secure until I reached the bottom. The mountain could not be climbed through here, I concluded.

It was time to bathe. The sweat and body oil from two days of heat and humidity clung to my skin like basting fat on a warm piece of meat. I boiled two gallons of water, let it cool, and then washed myself. *Ahh, that glorious feeling of cleanliness.*

"What's this?" I mumbled, working the glycerine soap through my left armpit.

I grabbed a mirror.

A tick!

As small as a mustard seed and nearly as red as a drop of blood. There was another one on my stomach, below my navel. And another on my leg. Two more on my neck. *Oh hell, this is all I need.*

Did I pick them up in the ravine? Or had they been with me for two days, ever since I grabbed the shovel and headed inland? I knew what they were. *Pinolíos,* the locals call them. I'd run into them before along rivers farther north and in some of the mountains near Mexico's frontera.

I tweezered them off, dabbed the bites with alcohol, then reconsidered my assault on the mountain. Years ago, to the north, I entered a monte where the pinolíos were as thick as mosquitoes on the Alaskan tundra. I came out of those woods with over fifty ticks on me. It took nearly three hours to pluck them off. I was in no mood to repeat that experience.

I fished for my dinner and was rewarded with another bass. In the afternoon (the sun had already dipped behind La Viuda by 3:30 P.M.) I sat on my aluminum folding chair, watching clouds drift over the mountain and glassing the birds that came to the trees.

A greenish blue motmot, its double tail looking like long exclamation marks, lit within twenty feet of me. About a hundred feet away, a Mexican squirrel cuckoo worked the bark of a tree as if stapled firmly to it. Now and then brown jays swooped into the trees above me and screamed: *Get the hell out of here, you foreigner, you pilgrim!*

I was surprised when I spotted three collared plovers busy at the edge of the sandbar behind me. These birds are not common in this region, preferring instead to keep farther south. The plovers' sharp *tseeerr* call moved weakly over the sand, and they seemed not the least concerned that I sat within a few yards of them.

Throughout the afternoon the soft coos of different species of doves filtered through the woods. I listened to the meditative white-tipped dove, the resonating red-billed pigeon, the rueful Inca and common ground doves, the poignant white-winged dove, and the mourning dove, whose coo needs no further description. At about four o'clock a small dove landed on the sand not more than twenty feet beyond the tent. It was a blue ground dove, a bird I had long hoped to see. After drinking, it cooed a hollow *whooop,* then flew quickly back into the deeper monte.

My journal was on my lap, its pages filling quickly with thoughts: *The scientist finds a place and wants to examine its objects; the writer finds a place and wants to examine the experience.*

Throughout the afternoon I watched the birds and clouds and listened to the wind blowing through the trees. There was a melancholy sound to the breeze. Or maybe the soft swaying of the tree limbs and the way the currents came in gentle modulating waves produced a cathexis of sorts, its center dwelling in that part of mind that remembers youth and family and times when the world seemed innocent.

Was the world really more innocent, or was it just the eyes through which it was seen that assayed it as such? A little of both, I assume.

The day grew old. Though I could not see it, its faithful fires burning mindlessly with no knowledge of how we depend on it, the sun delivered its diminuendo, a harmony of colors wafting over the mountain and into the clouds, a chromatic waning from yellow to orange to red to pink to gray to black.

I stood at the water's edge, grown old once more. If I could but reach for a minute into the past, then where would I go? To see my parents when they were young, to talk to my grandfather about el monte verde, to play with my children when they were babies, to know the joys of running hard, to see the world as it was before our avarice overwhelmed us and our technologies smothered us?

I withdrew to my chair by the campfire, and I played my guitar softly and watched the bluish red flame evanesce into timid yellow. Sometimes songs need no lyrics for they speak more clearly without them. The notes and chords express their own thoughts, their own feelings. There is often more in the song without the words than the poet can say with them.

At last the night settled quietly into the valley of the big river. Though the mountain loomed over me, it remained distant and unknown, like all other worlds near and far. The fire cooled to a few glowing embers, and stars emerged in all their fullness. I remained seated, staring at that colossal black mass that seemed to float above me—that immense scotoma through which the stars had no power.

Later, as I lay on my sleeping bag looking through the tent's nylon mesh door, I watched the stars as they appeared to move across the heavens. A frog of some sort grunted near the water. And a meteor scratched the sky for but an instant. Like all life, I guess.

The Fifth Day

In that moment of crepuscular stillness, when even the birds have yet to awaken, and the dawn is but an eye peeking lazily from afar, I sat quietly—eating toasted bread and watching a line of clouds gathering above me. *Today I will try the mountain again,* I told myself mentally. And a pair of chachalacas blew their abrasive trumpets from the trees lining the river's eastern bank, as if to herald my decision. A few minutes later the collared plovers reappeared, but they stayed for less than a minute.

I stood and walked to the river's edge and watched the opposite bank unveiled from beneath shadows cast from the cerros to the east. Something moved to my left about thirty yards away. I turned to see a large coati ambling up to the river, its pointed snout sniffing the sand, its tail erect as a flagpole and ringed alternately with russet browns and tarnished blacks.

Slowly, I retracted into a squatting ball and watched the old male drink. He dropped his tail, then propped it straight up again. He paused, sniffed the air, drank some more, sniffed the air, drank some more, and scratched his right ear with his right hind leg like a dog. Then he caught sight of me.

"Good morning," I said.
The coati's eyes grew wide.
"Drink up, my friend."
The coati whirled to face me.
"Now, now, be calm."
A strange barking sound. A blur of russet brown under silver-tipped fur. And into the woods. The crashing of branches then silence.

With the sun still sequestered behind the high cerros to the east, I prepared for the climb. I purified four quarts of water for my two two-quart canteens. I stuck ten homemade fruit-nut bars (oatmeal, raisins, dried dates, walnuts, and syrup) into my pack, a can of sardines, some little boxes of raisins, a jar of peanut butter, some packets of melba toast, my webbed nylon hammock, binoculars, rain parka, an extra cotton shirt, a couple of blue bandanas, my machete, three twelve gauge signal flares, some nylon parachute cord, the first aid kit, the mosquito netting; and I slung the shotgun over my shoulder.

I walked east for about fifty yards then entered the woods, carefully avoiding the plants in case pinolíos were clinging to them. Soon I found a small game trail that, to my surprise, opened into a large wash. The wash was like a tunnel, twenty yards across, enveloped by the canopies of limoncillos and other large trees bordering its edges, and with hundreds of smooth boulders strewn along its course like so many abandoned gray watermelons and brown cantaloupes.

The walking was relatively easy. I stepped from smooth boulder to smooth boulder, going up and up and farther into that dark tunnel. Within a few minutes, I had advanced at least the three hundred feet upward that had taken me an hour when I scaled the rooted ravine. But, *my luck*, the wash's easy, and not particularly steep, climb began deteriorating after I'd advanced three hundred feet farther—or at about six hundred feet. Several immense tree trunks traversed the path, their leafless limbs projecting chaotically outward and whetted by their own decay. I couldn't climb over them; I couldn't crawl under them; I couldn't squeeze by them. So I pulled out my machete and hacked my way through, gooey sweat exuding from flesh immersed in villainous humidity. It took me twenty minutes to get past each tree, and there were four of them within a stretch of about three hundred feet.

I paused and hung my pack from one of the limbs, then removed my hat and sweat-logged bandana and shirt, and sat on one of the watermelon-sized boulders and drank nearly a quart of water.

A long weary look upward. The ravine was littered with more dead trees. It seemed from my perspective as if the forest had become suddenly brown, with endless tree trunks stacked like a massive set of pickup sticks waiting to be carefully disengaged, lest they all give way in one colossal crash—on top of me.

Thunder!

It was close. And loud.

More thunder!

It wasn't a panic, but it was a grave concern. If it was already raining atop the mountain, then within minutes walls of water might sweep down the many washes that escalated its slopes. I knew I was in danger. I cursed myself for not having paid attention to the low-hanging clouds of the morning. Then suddenly, like a spigot abruptly turned on, the rain plummeted down on the dry forest and into the wash. I moved from one boulder to another and took a hard fall on the slippery melon rocks. Quickly, I regained my footing and worked my way to the edge of the wash. Grabbing onto exposed roots, I climbed out of that giant gully and ran onto a rocky outcrop, my heart in my throat.

A bolt of lightning slammed into the forest not more than seventy-five yards from where I sat. A second of total deafness followed by high-pitched tinnitus. Clumsily, I pulled on the nylon parka and sat, knees crammed against chest, sweat fermenting against rancid skin, the rain pummeling the earth around me. For twenty minutes, at least. But just as quickly as the spigot had opened, it closed.

I waited another minute, then stood and looked around and carefully climbed off the outcrop—and accidentally stepped into a viscous mush of soil and leaves. All around me came the tapping sounds from trees still raining their excess onto the forest's floor. Then like a flashbulb juiced with current, the sun broke.

A wave of humid heat rolled through the forest. I found shade, removed my parka, drank from my canteen, and tried to wipe the sweat off my face and onto my shirt. But my shirt was soaking wet, as was the spare in my pack. (Walk into a shower fully clothed, then step into mud, then with your clothes still on spend an hour in a sauna—in case you're wondering what it was like.)

A reverberating noise began rumbling through the forest, a steady roar like a jet taxing across the tarmac. I moved toward the sound and when I reached its source I stood in awe. Water mixed with melting brown earth and dismembered tree limbs churned through the wash. No doubt, every gulch, ravine, and gutter that webbed the mountain's slope was, at that instant, as gagged and rabid as the channel in front of me. And soon the gullies and gorges at the bottom would be choked as well. And the runoff would sweep into the river and join the rain spilling from each cerro that lay beneath the shower's path. Lasting but a moment, coming in a flash, and disappearing in a wink.

Okay, if I have to, I'll just stay put until the wash clears.

I sat on a flat rock still wet from the rain, exhausted by the humidity and weakened by the heat. I fished out the plastic bag filled with fruit-nut bars. Four bars later, I opened the sardine can and consumed its contents like a man who had gone without food for days. I drank the salty juice, licked the can clean, then removed my clothes and hung them out, not so much to let them dry as to free myself of the soggy weight.

I was about to hang my hammock between two trees when I noticed a sudden lull in the rushing water. What followed came quickly. The rampage of mud and churning torrents lessened within a few minutes to a mere trickle. I waited another few minutes until the trickle fizzled out completely. The clouds were gone. The sun was shining brightly. I got dressed and reentered the wash.

Back at camp I filled a two-gallon bucket at the river, poured a capful of bleach into it, and covered my body with thick glycerine suds.

I looked up at the mountain. The mountain stared down at me.

"Who do you think you are?" I growled.

And a peculiar feeling came over me. As if someone was saying, "Who do you think *you* are?"

Shoulders slumped, I said nothing more.

An hour later I was sitting on my aluminum chair under heavy shade. Zeiss binoculars dangled from my neck. A tin cup filled with steaming coffee stood next to me on a table fashioned from pieces of driftwood. The cast-iron Dutch oven was stewing potatoes, carrots, onions, and chile. A pair of red-billed pigeons balanced on the leafless limb of a tall tree a hundred feet in front of me. A gray-headed kite was poised at the apex of a lightning-charred trunk some sixty yards behind me. Now and then a breeze worked between the cerros and onto the river, otherwise quiet and still. A good and tranquil place—to think again on how we have come to embrace the idea that quality is quantity and that all things are but objects set forth to sate our needs.

I wonder if our "environmental crisis" is less a biological dilemma than it is a psychocultural predicament? We seem prone, of late, to want to cure our environmental woes by relying strictly on science, whether as a means of research or for teaching or even as a form of warning others about the ills facing our planet. But how successful is this tactic?

In *The Natural Alien,* philosopher and biologist Neil Evernden suggests that strict adherence to empirical rhetoric may have shortcomings that were not apparent when first employed:

> It is now possible simply to show the man in the street what's in it for him. By excising emotion and concentrating on numbers the environmentalist can show even the disinterested that it is prudent, economic, to retain a particular mountain in its present state. And since economics in this broad sense is believed to be fundamental to everyone's well-being, what was formerly a minority concern becomes a cause for all. We must protect and/or wisely manage our natural resources, because if we do not we may compromise our standard of living. (9)

I think of Rachel Carson's *Silent Spring,* published in 1962, as an example of the limitations of resolute empirical argument. Carson's book was a valiant effort emphasizing sound, empirically based data as a means of interpreting and rectifying the problem of agricultural pesticide abuse in nature. The book did in fact inspire us to divest ourselves of the chlorinated hydrocarbon insecticides like DDT and thus to save the bald eagle and other threatened birds. But just as quickly we embraced organophosphates, derivatives of German nerve gases, and in the interim we have nearly wiped out our pollinating insects, according to Stephen Buchmann and Gary Nabhan in *Our Forgotten Pollinators.* Scientific warnings, despite their cold hard facts, seem not to have caused us to change our behavior.

The sky had been washed clean by the shower earlier in the day. Now it was filling anew with that yellow-gray overcast, a firmament grown immune to the baptism of a summer's rain. But I noticed now that the overcast looked more like smoke, and it appeared to be coming from behind the mountain.

As evening approached, the twilight seemed reluctant to give way to the blackness of night. I had kept the tiny fire going throughout the afternoon, enjoying the rhythmic crackling of dry wood, the sweet smells of burning resins. And yes, contributing to the haze above. As I stood at the river's edge holding a delicate line that disappeared on the water's surface, I tried to memorize the sunset. It seemed to stand still and yet change, all at the same time. Slowly, I reached out my hand and for an instant it extended far into the cosmos. For a long short moment we stood as one—the water and sand and the sky and heavens united through tenuous strands of flesh and spirit woven delicately by feelings and hopes and dreams that found no boundaries or distances or even time, a union immeasurable in its continuum but real nonetheless.

The Sixth Day

Daylight came as if the night's interlude still lay quietly blanketed over it. Each day I was becoming more at ease in this place. I walked to the river's edge and stood watching torpid water mingle with the sand and small pebbles lining the little beach. Above me the stars, one by one, liquefied within pink and golden hues glowing steadily brighter in the morning's calm. At last a bird whistled unpretentiously somewhere behind the rampart of tall trees leaning over the camp and edging the sand. Back at my makeshift table I prepared oatmeal with water heated in a blue enameled pot set over the small fire. I dabbed three slices of melba toast with peanut butter and sliced a mango. But I did not fish that day.

At first, I thought—as I sat voicelessly greeting the morning and eating my breakfast—that I would do nothing. *A day of rest and relaxation with no climbing or hiking.* But even as I thought to sit still, I found myself repacking my backpack—my journal, my shirts, my first aid kit, some food, the sleeping bag, and my ultra-lightweight mesh hammock. Even as I debated whether or not to reclimb the wash, I purified enough water to fill my two canteens. Even as I knew the heat would return in full, I set out from camp and found my way back into the forest.

I'd climbed the wash for about two hundred feet when a groping sun first showed above the cerros to the east. I sat and removed my gloves and popped the contents of a little box of raisins into my mouth. Back at camp, I'd mixed a pack of Gatorade into one of the canteens. As I scanned the wash above me, I drank liberally and made a mental note to pause frequently to replenish my electrolytes. The quiet persisted, save for dull bootsteps on smooth, melon rocks.

On my third rest stop, as I sat holding the opened canteen on my lap and looking upward into the wash, I noticed something moving along the top of one of the downed tree trunks. Most of the trunks that had straddled the wash the day before were, as a result of the storm, now lying lengthwise, the massive logs asleep again and waiting to be reawakened by another brief surge of energy. The moving object blended so perfectly with the trunks that it seemed to be melting in and out of them. It hopped from a trunk about a hundred feet above me on my right to a trunk on my left that came to within ten feet overhead.

An ocelot!

Its tawny coat was speckled with nickel-sized rosettes, slate black like the woodpecker holes pockmarking the fallen trees. It moved with the grace of a prima ballerina—-musically fluid movements in diminished tones and subdued kinesis, an organic decrescendo that abated into utter stillness.

I sat motionless. It had not seen me sitting almost directly below it until it reached the very tip of the log. There seemed no fear in its eyes, perhaps because there was no evil in mine. It sat on its haunches watching me, licking its whiskers and gingerly readjusting its position—trying to figure out what I was. It swooshed its tail but stayed seated. In all fairness, I should add that the closeness of this encounter was not necessarily astounding. Ocelots are quite common here and sightings are frequent and, because of the dense foliage, usually at very close range. In fact, at another locale marked by thick vegetation, Laguna Atascosa National Wildlife Refuge in South Texas, my son, Jason, and I came to within spitting range of a large grayish ocelot. That experience, however, was tainted because the cat was wearing a radio collar, and though it was competely wild, the cumbersome technological artifact dangling from its neck reduced the thrill of seeing it considerably.

Biting flies were buzzing around me. One lit on my cheek, another on my neck. I felt stabbing proboscises penetrating epidermal and dermal flesh, across tiny nerves and into the red wine of warm, erythrocytic *sangre*. I dared not move, but at last I could suffer no more. The second I swished the flies away, the cat's eyes tensed; then it turned and melted into the trunks and limbs that lay in disordered boxcar formation along the wash.

I continued climbing, sweating into a fresh blue bandana wrapped around my forehead, the underside of my pack gummy with perspiration, the shotgun slung loosely over my shoulder, my gloves on, the rim of my hat sprayed now with insect repellent. And wondering—*what will I do when I reach the top of the wash?*

Thirty minutes later and I was there. The wash shriveled into two tiny, root-ridden ravines—not unlike that first ravine I had entered a few days before. I glanced downward. It seemed a lot steeper from this angle than it had coming up. I worked my way left, to the south, and found a thin game trail that angled upward between rocks and shrubs and allowed me to gain another two hundred feet in elevation. It opened onto a shelf about twenty yards wide and circling southward.

I climbed a boulder the size of a pickup truck and stood to look about. From this perspective I could tell that I had scaled the mountain about halfway, perhaps a little more. The summit loomed high over me. Ultra dense monte rose above the shelf for hundreds of feet, where it bonded with a great vertical rock. This was the eastern side of La Viuda. On the northern side—the side seen from don Miguel and doña María's home—the dense monte snailed unbroken above the widow's two solemn eyes on up to the summit.

I decided to follow the shelf and see if it would lead me to the mountain's southern face. The walk proceeded leisurely, the sun directly above, a steady southeasterly breeze buffeting the low shrubs covering the shelf like woody grass mown to exactly one foot in height. I pursued a maze of narrow game trails meandering haphazardly on this limestone table, the small dirt patches atop it inscribed with deer and javelina tracks, ocelot and bobcat tracks, coyote tracks, skunk tracks, coati tracks. *And*—I stooped to inspect a hair-ridden dropping ten inches long—*lion sign.* Cougar probably. Maybe a jaguar? Both inhabit this remote region.

Studying the ground, I spotted the cat's four-inch tracks. *El león* had done its business then bounded up the mountain.

I rolled the dropping over with a small stick. The scat was fresh, not more than twelve hours old. *Are you watching me?* I wondered, perusing the surrounding monte.

An hour later I reached the southeastern flang of the mountain. Here, a divergence of shrub-covered, rocky outcroppings created a basin about three hundred yards wide and at least four hundred feet deep. Within it, at that great confluence of gravitational forces, the earthbound energies of unrestrainable waters had carved out another wash. From where I stood it seemed but a slender brown snake scaled with thousands of smooth boulders and intertwined within a labyrinth of edematous trees, their bloated trunks and limbs covering an earth sans shrubs and grass.

Through my binoculars I could tell that this wash was as big as the one I had climbed up, if not bigger.

It was time to refigure my ascent. The shelf disappeared at the edges of this angling basin. I could see that it began again on the far side. Reaching that other side would mean a forced probe into the basin's depths. Hundreds of feet down, then hundreds of feet back up. I was low on water. I was tired. So I looked around for a place to rest and think.

Above me about fifty feet I spotted a ledge some twenty feet wide and maybe thirty yards long. Water was trickling down from the ledge over the limestone, the tiny stream no wider than a pencil. Climbing through nearly impenetrable brush, I reached the ledge, arms scratched, and once again drenched in sweat. As luck would have it, I found scraped into the rock a small pool of water about the size of a washtub . . . *a gift from the mountain to its occupants.*

My two canteens refilled, I sat on a nearby boulder that looked like a king-sized bed nudged against the back of the little ledge. I gazed into the sloping basin, catching the stiff breezes with my body and relishing the mountain's beauty. I had hoped to see if I could spot the source of that yellowish-gray smoke I had seen the day before. But I had seen no smoke during my ascent up the wash, nor on my hike along La Viuda's shoulder.

Evening. The sun had long since dipped behind the mountain. I had napped for at least an hour. When I awoke I ate a couple of boxes of raisins and two fruit-nut bars, and I brewed some coffee. I would camp here tonight.

There was nothing to hook my lightweight hammock onto so I folded it and laid it on the king bed boulder as a pillow on top of my sleeping bag, and then sat and looked into the little basin, the night creeping steadily into it. Far to the east I saw slivers of lightning jettisoned from distant clouds. Minutes later the sounds of dull bass drums rolled across the land. As long as the storm stayed far away, I would be okay.

In my right peripheral vision, I caught a sweeping blackness moving out of the little basin. I turned quickly. The swarming mass—a fluid cloud erupting from below me—grew larger. It came at me with intense speed, an amoebic blob rising and swelling. The cloud engulfed me. I jumped off the king bed boulder and hid behind it as thousands of bats, their wings slapping the air loudly, rushed past me. Instantly, I was deluged by a horrific smell, alkaloidal and putrid. I pressed my nose into the crook of my arm, then crunched my body into as small a shape as I could. The fulminating cloud, whirling inches above me, seemed endless. Then it was gone. The great airborne amoeba, frenzied pseudopods spurting outward from its fleshly core, dwindled into a small, black, coagulated dot.

I stood. The smell lingered for another five minutes, then it too disappeared. I checked my sleeping bag for guano, but it was unscathed.

I spent the next fifteen minutes, as the last of the light evaporated, trying to figure a way to support my mosquito net over my sleeping bag. But it was impossible. Anyway, there didn't seem to be any mosquitoes at this altitude. So I turned my attention to building a fire. When the sticks and dry leaves caught, I lay on the sleeping bag and watched the flame's flickering light dance against the rocks.

It was a long time before I finally fell asleep. The nap, the two cups of coffee, and perhaps the possibility of the bats deciding to return early kept me awake. I added more wood to the fire and spent the time writing in my journal.

Some environmental scholars have adopted the word *anthropocentric* (defined in *Merriam Webster's* tenth collegiate edition as "interpreting or regarding the world in terms of human values and experiences") as a way to explain the callous character of humans toward the earth. But, I wonder, how else are humans to interpret the world? Is not the lion felinocentric, or the wolf caninocentric? Are we not to expect humans then to be anthropocentric? And yet, we have—no reasonable person would deny this—desecrated much of the earth, not just for humans but for all animals and plants. I think the words *values* and *experiences* in the aforegoing definition are key to understanding the ethic we have embraced. I therefore suggest another word that I believe more accurately defines the modern human's worldview. That word is autodiocentric. *Self-god-centered.*

But then *how* did we become autodiocentric? How did we come to think of ourselves as gods?

In a book entitled *The Religion of Technology,* historian David Noble presents an interesting explanation of one step (a recent step) in our evolution toward perceiving ourselves as deities. Noble analyzes a story with which we are all familiar: In the beginning we were perfect. But through guile and temptation we lost our perfection, and we have been forced to live lives of endless toil and pain. However—and this is the important part—we can regain our perfection through *faith and good works*. Remember that the fundamental idea in the story is that we *were* perfect and that we can *regain* perfection through faith and through good works. Of the two components, the more important is faith. But faith, it emerged, could be both strengthened and enhanced by our works. (Noble credits this insight to a Cistercian abbot of the Middle Ages who lived in Calabria and whose name was Joachim of Fiore.) As a society we began to concentrate on developing our good works so that we could regain our perfection. At first, Noble says, we called our good works "the useful arts." Later they were called "the mechanical arts." Today we call them "technology"—and *science*.

Noble asserts that over time technology (and science) became the embodiment of the story itself. Technology became a corporeal path toward perfection. Technology and science replaced the God of our story and became gods of our reality:

> With Hugh [of St. Victor] the monastic reconception of the useful arts was fully articulated as a means of reunion with God, a theme sustained in the thirteenth century by Michael Scot, who held that "the primary purpose of the human sciences is to restore fallen man to his prelapsarian position," and by Franciscan friar Bonaventura, who likewise "sanctified the mechanical arts and placed them in the context of knowledge whose source and goal is the light of God." Such work—by a canon, a layman, and a mendicant friar—not only further ratified the moral virtuousness of the useful arts but also helped to spread monastic ideas beyond the cloister, fostering in Europe a unique emotional commitment to machinery, grounded upon an "acceptance of mechanisms as aids to the spiritual life." (20)

Humans, science and technology. The trinity of modern men and women, their new road toward perfection. You hear it now almost daily: *Science will save us. Don't worry about the problems we face; technology will see us through and save the day.* So we hasten our return to perfection (or our attainment of it, depending on one's personal beliefs) by worshiping our science, by bowing to our technology, and by our own self-deification.

A pauraque whistled but a few yards from my bed. *Whoop, whoop, wheeooo.* To the east, I could still see oscillating flashes of lightning. But they were too weak to produce enough thunder to carry the distance. I placed my journal back inside a pocket I reserve for it in my backpack, and I lay back on my sleeping bag and searched the heavens. How I wished my family could have been there with me. My wife and sons, my parents, my sister and her husband, my grandparents, aunts and uncles and cousins. The way it used to be, long ago. One more grand picnic. Like the kind we'd have on Easter Sunday.

The Seventh Day

A tachycardic flutter of ten thousand wings woke me two hours before sunrise. This time the bats did not swoop as low over the rocks as they had the previous evening. Still, their rank smell poured heavily onto the narrow shelf, a fetid vapor as robust as the cohesion of wing beats was loud. It was a restless night. Nonetheless, sometime after the bats returned—thirty minutes later or thereabouts—I drifted into a deep sleep, a dream-filled hour and a half reliving life long removed from consciousness. For me those dreams always begin with a song. When I first began having them, in my mid-thirties, I'd awake trembling and in a state of profound mourning. That graphic feeling of loss, its lucidity brought forth in colors backdropped by sounds—the music and voices of times ensconced in the past—burrowed its way into my bones. I'd walk from room to room in the dark predawn hours, the loneliest man on earth, during those moments when clocks grind down, turning seconds into minutes, and minutes into hours.

The songs are not *my* songs, not personal songs, but songs of the generations—the music of youth, and growing up and discovering life and love. And that night on the little ledge, for whatever reason chosen by that other me—that sentient soul housed somewhere within this blending of flesh and bone—came the music of the early 1970s trio, Emerson, Lake & Palmer: "He was a lucky man, he was . . ."

So where do you go when you're sitting on a large king bed boulder pressed against the side of a mountain—the past but another galaxy, whirling somewhere far away? *Nowhere.* You must endure what cannot be altered. So I sat and told myself that I should go forward. There is only one alternative, and I was not ready for that.

The rising sun broke the dream's spell. Lighted hands reached across the horizon thumbing their way into my eyes. It was only a dream. I was walking in the early morning, a boy filled with wonder, smelling the dewy earth, surrounded by thick monte and talking to my father, who was still a young man.

I brewed some coffee, ate melba toast and peanut butter, then set out to explore—to see if there was a way across the basin and onto the south side of the mountain. While at the level of the smaller rocky shelf, I reexamined a patch of moist earth that I had inspected the day before, within a few feet of the small pool that had fed my canteens. The previous day, the moist earth patch had been free of tracks. Today it clearly showed the paw marks of a large cat. Within a few yards of where I had spent the night, a beast with paws measuring something over four inches in diameter had walked. Had it wanted me, it could easily have had me. But it did not want me. It was only curious. I was not concerned. In fact, I was pleased to be the object of such regard.

Back at my spike camp I downed a small box of raisins, repacked my backpack, then set out—south by southwest. Past the moist earth patch, for one last look at those beautiful tracks. Then onto a game trail that climbed down into the basin. It was a good path. Down and up, down and sideways, then down and down and down, the path taking the easiest route the animals that made it could find.

All the while, calls and whistles from countless birds sifted up from the basin. I stopped cold when a rufescent tinamou walked out in front of me not more than fifteen feet away. That sighting alone made the trip worth it. Later on, as I was about halfway into the basin, I spotted a mottled owl, its frigid stare accented sternly by a V-notch of white feathers above its eyes.

Down and down, until I could no longer see the basin's ridges. The underbrush became sparse. Magnificent trees with barrel-sized black trunks that pressed ponderous limbs into one another surrounded me. Organic debris, soft and wet, cushioned my footsteps. *Quiet* . . . ultra noiseless, soundless quiet. And cool.

The temperature had dipped by at least ten degrees when I reached the basin's bottom. I sat within the serpentine wash that I had first seen from atop the ridge. I drank the last of one canteen of water. Then it occurred to me: *Now you'll have to climb up and out of here.* I had only one water-filled canteen left. What if there was no water on the south side of the mountain?

I rested for about twenty minutes, eating melba toast dabbed with peanut butter, a box of raisins, and a small can of mixed fruit—contemplating my next move. I considered simply walking down the wash and then trying to find a way back to my river camp. But it was still morning, and I *wanted* to see the south side of the mountain, as mysterious to me as the back of the moon. From that unknown world I might find a way to the summit. So I began climbing. For about three hundred feet the trek was amiable. Shadows darkened the ground and kept the area cool.

As I rounded a mammoth tree, at least fifty feet tall with indolent limbs veering laterally, their individual weights measured, no doubt, in tons, I detected movement among some fallen leaves. A large green snake scaled its way over the foliage, a collage of iridescent colors—blue, green, silver, purple—reflecting off its back in the shifting light. When it spotted me, it raced into a clump of shrubs and then worked its way into a hole fashioned by several limestone rocks.

I proceeded cautiously after spotting that snake. It did not look venomous. But if one snake was out, then others would be also. Fer-de-lance and coral and an aggressive species of rattler are known to inhabit the area.

The shaded slope soon became a confused addle of broken limbs and snapped trunks. This was the side where the winds hit hardest. In one spot it looked as if a tornado had flogged the mountain, uprooting plants from its thin soils like a razor removing a beard.

I bargained my way through the entanglements by paying dearly in consumed water and energy. Finally, I reached the rocky ridge that formed the southern rim of the little basin. There, under a small tree forever hunched by frequent gales, I rested, allowing two drenched shirts to dry on branches held against steady breezes. I ate a small pack of mixed nuts, some melba toast, two more little boxes of raisins. And brought my remaining water-filled canteen to less than half its contents.

I had undershot the ledge that extended from the other side of the basin and continued southward, the same ledge I'd walked the day before. So I climbed another hundred feet to reach it. Within twenty minutes I was on the south side of the mountain.

Here dwarfed trees, their canopies warped by persistent winds, lined the mountain. I had managed, in a day and a half to climb only halfway. I was tired, feet cramping, sweat sticking to my underarms and along my back, and I needed water—but inside, from that centermost place of being, as happy as a child encountering something never before seen.

I looked up into a veil of thin clouds exuding from two great rocks.

One was part of the titanic monolith that touched the sky on the eastern slope; the other, not quite as large, was distinctly crenulated. I placed my pack on the ground and removed my hat, knowing that it was time to face reality. Reaching the summit looked hopeless. "There it is," I mumbled. *So close and yet . . .*

I continued westward, one canteen half full, the other empty. Ten minutes later I stopped when I noticed a sliver of white smoke rising out of the forest in the distance. I put my binoculars to my eyes, but dropped them back on my chest in disbelief, perhaps needing an unaided view in order to accept what I was seeing. Again, the binoculars came up, and I panned the forest left to right.

It was about eight or ten miles away, but even so I could see several large trucks parked alongside piles of logs shaped like small pyramids. The smoke was coming from the edges of the clear-cut. The logging was obviously moving toward me, and thus toward the mountain.

I sat and watched for nearly an hour. *Is there no place to go and be free of this sort of thing?* I wondered. I recalled a conversation with an old friend who told me: "I don't worry any more about what's happening to the earth, because there's nothing I can do about it." I thought at that moment that he had never done anything to begin with, and that ceasing to worry about it was simply an excuse to continue doing nothing.

But then what could *I* do about all of this? I recalled Juan and don Miguel's lament that the people who were denuding the forest had no right to be on the land; that they were, in fact, trespassing, and what documents they possessed were forged. At the same time I hated myself for allowing anger to rise up within me and destroy the beauty of what I had experienced so far. But the anger remained, a sick feeling I have unfortunately become accustomed to over the years.

I continued walking and by early afternoon I'd reached the far westward side of the mountain's southern face. I was anxious to climb higher, more so now to see the clear-cutting to the south than to reach the summit. But there were no game paths or rocky ridges that might be followed like some magic path to the top. I examined every possibility. At the end of the ledge, where it crumbled into a steep slide of gravely scree, I found an eroded cut zigzagging upward. I followed the cut for about a hundred and fifty feet. But it ended abruptly at a bulwark of chest-high thorny shrubs. For several minutes I watched the summit, wondering what I would have found there, and trying not to turn and look behind me, at the smoke rising off the forest floor.

There was no way directly down from where I was standing. So I retraced my steps along the ledge back toward the little valley—pausing frequently to gaze through my binoculars at the logging to the south, my heart sinking deeper, the disgust and sadness growing steadily within.

I had found no water. So I had two options. Upon reaching the basin, I could climb down then up again and refill my canteens at the tiny pool from which I had claimed water the day before. Or I could follow the basin to the bottom of the mountain, hoping to find a source of water on the trek back to my river camp.

The winds along the southern slope waned as the afternoon aged. At mid-afternoon I reached the rocky rim that formed the little basin's southern border. The sky remained cloudless, save for distant chalk marks to the north. Instead of following the same route I had used to climb out of the basin, I decided to climb up the rocky rim by about two hundred feet, then descend along a line of trees that I thought—hoped—seemed to follow a ravine into the large wash at the basin's center. In effect, I was hoping to sidetrack the mayhem of fallen trees and thorny shrubs I'd encountered on the way up, and perhaps find water along the route.

But upon reaching the point where I planned to drop into the basin, I realized that no ravine underscored the tree line. Three or four abreast, the tall trees themselves bent downward like a green waterfall tumbling into the wash far below.

The walk was unfettered; I wish my thoughts could have been the same. A few minutes into the descent, I noticed that the basin's rocky border had restrained the winds I had encountered on the ledge. I stopped and took a deep breath. But the mired images of smoke and of logs stacked in immense piles were still vivid and unyielding, as if my binoculars had not been removed from my eyes.

The mountain was now blocking the afternoon sun, and the tall trees' shade joined the mountain's shadow to turn the path into a tenebrous tunnel. The leaf-covered ground grew darker, the trees larger, as I continued into the basin.

Yet despite the dimness of light, I froze the instant I saw it. Its geometry, sharp angles out of place in a maze otherwise all curvature, caught my eye. Out of place, yes, and yet as much a part of the mountain as the rocks, shrubs and trees that clothed it. The color of dried limbs and dead leaves and of moss over pebbles. The little dwelling stood as quiet as a tombstone, and as forgotten as an unmarked grave.

It was at the edge of the line of trees, their shadows burying it in darkness. I approached cautiously. But if there was anyone around, it was only a ghost or two.

The rock dwelling stepped off at fourteen by twelve feet, remnants of its stick roof decaying in the small confines of its interior. Cottony spiderwebs centered by marble-sized brown bodies, each fuzzy orb supporting six spindly legs, draped its walls. A brooding brown lizard, eight armored inches from snout to tail's tip, wedged in between two of the south wall's rocks. A centipede, six inches of polished black with pumpkin-orange legs, squeezed flatly between two rocks on the east face. Black rodent droppings formed a mat at the crumbling door. Owl pellets, old and new, were piled in the northeast corner. A translucent segment of dried, discarded snakeskin lay wrapped between some of the fallen wall rocks. A small tree—the progeny of its mother above—grew from out of the southeast corner.

Then I saw the other one. Farther down, thirty yards away; a fallen branch as big around as a truck tire had crushed it. Even before I started pacing it off, I knew this second dwelling would also measure twelve by fourteen feet.

Looking down along the line of husky trees and then at the woods bordering them, I saw no other dwellings.

The Earth People? I mused. But, of course, two small huts could not support a band. Perhaps other human-made vestiges lay nearby buried beneath rotting organic rubble. I took a quick look around, but found nothing to suggest that scenario. These were nothing more than squatter's huts—abandoned years ago, as is their wont, when the builder's urge to reside elsewhere grows strong.

I could live here. Why couldn't I live here? Who is it that proclaims where I must live? Who sets the rules? I recalled the words of C. S. Lewis: "Man's power over Nature means the power of some men over other men with Nature as the instrument."

But then was my wish any different from the wish of those who want to live wherever they choose, and who proclaim loudly that they can do with *their* land as they please?

I sat on the cool earth, my pack leaning against a broken tree limb, canteen in hand and staring at the first hut. Twelve by fourteen feet. Rocks and sticks. No electricity. No garage. No swimming pool. No satellite dish. No road winding up to it. Perhaps it depends on *how* one lives, I thought.

In a book called *Justice and the Earth,* law professor Eric Freyfogle writes:

> Wilderness is a legal as well as mental construct, and wilderness in the law means an area off limits to those who seek work. Wilderness, the federal statute says, is not just land "retaining its primeval character and influence, without permanent improvements or human habitation"; it is land "where the earth and its community of life are untrammeled by man, where man himself is a visitor who does not remain." (95)

But does that specificity suggest, in subtle ways, an acquiescence of mind, an implicit understanding that American ways of living cannot embrace the thought of nature as anything but an object or instrument? Perhaps our wilderness areas are less an affirmation of underlying good character than an admission of guilt.

And yet here in this quiet, shadowed place, people lived in apparent harmony with nature. They were as much wilderness as the trees and birds and other living things surrounding them. So then what is it that nature cannot afford? Perhaps it is gluttony, in whatever form, that is the true enemy of the earth. Wilderness then becomes a medicine that annuls our avaricious appetites.

I breathed in the quiet, wondering what it had been like to live here, even before the squatters came? Children's voices coalesced suddenly from within secluded chambers of my imagination, places where fantasy becomes nearly real. A little girl skipped in front of me, returning from a foray in the woods, her mother walking behind her, a basket of pitahaya fruit in her arms. The little girl said something to me, but it was not in Spanish. It was a tongue of *this* land and not some conqueror's language. I waved and she skipped on.

A rack of drying meat stood nearby. A stream of feathery smoke rose from a tiny fire but a few feet away. It smelled of food cooking and of closeness to the earth.

A man was walking up along the line of trees. He had a string of five fish draped over his nearly naked body. He smiled at the woman, then went about sorting the fish on a table made from fallen twigs and small branches.

Another long breath. *I could live here . . .*

As I descended into the basin I searched for more dwellings. But there were none. When I reached the rocky wash I decided to follow it down to the base of the mountain. My legs had begun cramping about halfway into the basin, a sign of electrolyte depletion. I briefly considered climbing up the other side of the basin to refill my canteens at the small pool. But my aching legs decided otherwise. There was nothing to do but go downward—hoping to find a source of water somewhere at the base of the wash.

I found some vines and hacked them with my machete, then drank a few drops of clear water from their cores. It was a trick an old friend named Dagoberto had taught me years before. The water kept my tongue moist and my mind off my thirst.

I moved slowly, cutting vines for water along the way. The sunlight fading. The wash more and more cavelike, with brutish trees holding long arthritic arms that reached out to grab unsuspecting prey foolish enough to enter these regions.

By late afternoon I was at the base of the mountain, the wash ending at a melon rock and timber graveyard. Here the stones were jumbled over and under splintered branches and decomposing logs, the remnants of proud trees that once gazed upon the earth from atop the mountain.

The wash I followed downward was much longer, though not as steep as the wash I had explored upward the day before. At its base this second wash broke into many small fingers—narrow channels, moss covered and grass lined. I chose the one that angled most sharply to my left, the one that seemed to offer the most direct route back to the river.

Night was minutes away. I could only guess at how far I must be from my base camp. Three or four miles?

I had barely entered the lower wash when the darkness rolled in like a waterless fog. It rose inertly from beneath the low shrubs, exuding a black gaseous film, rounding my legs then floating up weightlessly. At the same moment, the darkness fell from that thin sky that lives but inches above the trees. The blackness from below and from above fused in front of me, then entered my eyes as if an eclipse had suddenly formed within them.

I groped for my flashlight. *Don't tell me I didn't pack the damn thing* . . . Found it. And walked on following a paltry yellow beam that fuzzed randomly a few feet in front of me. One hour. Two hours. *I must be a long way off . . .*

The watercourse finally became too choked with shrubs and small trees to negotiate. The flashlight's beam began to fatigue. The trees and shrubs—*a jungle*—squeezed me, used up my energy, pushed me off course.

Another hour passed. Crazy with thirst. The flashlight's beam now at less than half strength. I should sit here and wait for morning. I'm lost. Hell, admit it, you're lost.

But I did not stop. I decided to keep going until the flashlight gave up. An hour passed. The flashlight was at quarter strength with no more than twenty minutes left of power. Soon I would have no choice but to sit and wait for the sun to come up. As long as I had light, I would keep moving.

A few minutes later I broke through. The trees gave way to sand, the quiet river but a few feet beyond. I had overshot my camp by about two hundred yards. In a state of utter exhaustion, I walked along the river's edge until I reached *home*.

I had a gallon of purified water in a plastic jug inside my tent.

I emptied two Gatorade packets into the jug and drank nearly the whole thing. Two Tylenol caplets went down with it. I pulled off my clothes, tossed them on the sand, walked naked into my tent. Feverish from dehydration and a little dizzy, I looked out the tent's mosquito-netted door flap. Sunrise was two or three hours away. I laid back, achy and angry at myself for having been so careless. And I fell asleep.

The Eighth Day

It was noon and I was sitting on the aluminum chair contemplating my failed attempt at the mountain's summit. I could have hired ten or twelve men and supplied them with chain saws to cut a path up the mountain from the rocky shelf. I could have told them to make a winding road, not too steep. Negotiate a comfortable trail . . . I could have brought in one of those all-terrain vehicles, the four wheelers that go *anywhere*. I could have driven up the mountain from the shelf, then stood on the summit and looked down, across the valleys, onto the river and far into the distance. Yes, I could probably have beaten the mountain. And yet, as I took my place on that highest point, it would have been difficult shielding my eyes from my own good works. Perhaps the smell of chain saw exhaust might still linger, as would the odor of gasoline and oil seeping out from my four-wheeled chariot.

I could have reached the very top. But once there, I would not have seen what I saw when I first began climbing the mountain. My new road would become a horrid scar of bony-white limestone, the topsoil washed into the river with the first rain; and the winds that rushed unencumbered through the cut would deplete the biomass on either side, the trees and shrubs withering without appeal. Yes, I could have climbed to the top, but at what cost?

Was it not better to walk the natural rocky shelf and live peacefully and enjoy the beauty of a mountain unmolested; and know that the summit was not something to be conquered but instead to be celebrated? And my life and all life was better because I stayed on a middle ground and did not force the mountain to submit because I insisted on reaching the very top—a place once attained forever lost. So from my camp I looked up, the mountain high above me remained beautiful and undefiled.

I took a long bath, still achy and tired, then hung my hammock between two trees for a nap. Around mid afternoon I got up and heated a can of vegetable soup in the Dutch oven, adding some of the red chile doña María had given me. I also made some tortillas de harina (Two cups of flower, a half cup of warm water, a pinch of salt, and a small scoop of shortening makes enough tortillas for two people or one hungry guy.) and I cooked them on my cast iron skillet. I was still feeling rundown, but the food helped renew my strength.

After eating I took a stroll along the narrow beach. And found a small log about four feet long, and lifted it carefully to peek underneath at hundreds of termites and a small centipede. I sat on the sand examining the furrows and passageways the termites had cut into the bottom of the log, and carefully keeping the centipede away from my hand. At first the termites' troughs seemed chaotic. But as I looked more closely, I realized there was a symmetry and logic to their diggings. Three or four straight channels followed by one that curved to the left or right—depending on the angle from which one viewed the log.

There were other logs lying nearby. But I had peeked under one and therefore knew, for the most part, what lay under the others. I could have picked them all up. I could have rationalized: *This knowledge is important to know. I should seek to discover what lies under the logs.* But then by pursuing discovery I would have destroyed the synchrony beneath *all* the logs. Was discovery so important that it superseded the needs and lives of the creatures of the logs? Should my desire to know supplant some other creature's need to live? And does my knowing more and more truly make me value more and more? For some, perhaps. But it seems that for too many others that knowledge leads only to a depraved obsession to control and mistreat.

I think of the words of Neil Evernden in *The Natural Alien:*

> [Objectivity] is not a simple term, although I am using it in the colloquial sense of that which is uninfluenced by personal feelings or motivations. To be objective, in this sense, is to be uninvolved—to be the neutral observer who is believed to be the most reliable guide to action. Since by this understanding the objective person is not personally committed, he has no vested interest in that which he views. Neither does he have any obligation towards it. He is to-

tally apart. Now while we may admire this stance as a means of gaining information, we normally do not appreciate it as a way of gaining information about ourselves. Going to a physician or psychologist is a very disconcerting experience, not just because it is strange or unknown, but because it is deeply offensive. Consider what it means to be treated as an object. (88)

Back at camp I took out my guitar. The music lifted my spirits. I played a progression starting in D major, leading to A minor then B flat major seventh. I added a melody to it, but gave up on the composition after a few minutes. Instead, I just jammed. A little blues. Some jazz. A piece by Bach à la Jethro Tull. Then some Ray Orbison: *Pretty woman, won't you pardon me? Pretty woman, I couldn't help but see that you look lonely, just like me* . . .

"Buenas."

I stopped in mid-strum when I heard the voice.

"Buenas tardes, señor. Escuchamos la música. Estábamos pescando aya, en el otro lado de esos árboles."

I grinned nervously. The two men were in a small wooden boat that looked handmade. They said they were fishing and that they heard the music. They were *puro Indio*. Smooth beardless faces, straight long black hair, dark tilting eyes, their skin the rich reddish brown of rosíos mesquite, rugged looking and yet handsome. They rowed the boat onto the beach and stepped out, smiling. I remained seated, guitar in hand.

Both men looked in their mid-thirties. I was struck by their warm smiles. I was smiling too—but thinking about the shotgun that was unloaded and in the tent.

"Estás pescando, señor?"

"No, I'm not fishing," I said. "I'm just here, spending some time alone."

Both men nodded. They didn't seem to be carrying any sort of weapons. No machetes or guns. One man wore faded black jeans and an old western shirt, blue and white striped, the left pocket torn off. The other man wore pants made from a purple polyester. His shirt was of khaki, old and stained. Both wore leather sandals and wide-brimmed straw hats. One man, the one in black jeans, had a rather prominent nose, the nasal spine protruding outward in a distinctive arc, perhaps a break never reset to heal properly. The other man's nose was narrow and pointed. I think the first man's nose would have looked like the second man's nose had he not broken it. Beyond the difference in their noses, there weren't any other major dissimilarities between the two. Perhaps they were brothers? They were nearly the same size, about five feet, eight inches.

"Gustan unas tortillas?" I asked.

The men smiled and nodded. So I stood and gave them each two tortillas de harina.

They sat on their haunches, eating quietly. I offered them water from one of my canteens. They declined. I sat down again, and—thinking this might be a good move—began strumming my guitar.

By nightfall we had a good fire going. As I had suspected, Jorge and Ricardo were brothers. Jorge wore the narrow nose and Ricardo the arched nose. They lived a few kilometers downriver at a small settlement where two more brothers, their respective wives and children, and the brothers' father and mother also lived. I wasn't nervous any more; in fact, I was glad for the company.

While I played the guitar, Ricardo and Jorge prepared some fish. We added potatoes, onions, tomato, garlic, chile. Then I made more tortillas de harina and brewed more coffee. We ate. We talked. I played my guitar.

"Ustedes gustan vivir aquí?" I asked.

"Sí, como no," said Jorge.

"Es muy pacífico," Ricardo added.

"How do you all live?"

I realized immediately my question was odd, a relic of the world I am forced to live in.

The brothers shrugged. Ricardo sipped his coffee contemplatively.

"We fish," Jorge said. "And we grow corn and vegetables." He paused, as if intuitively understanding that my question had suggested a frame of reference foreign from his. "We exist quietly, señor."

"It is a good life here," I said, wondering if the brothers would understand that I meant that the quality of their lives, in my opinion, was better in many respects than the quality of life in the world I come from.

But neither brother said anything. In the firelight, their dark faces seemed especially adept at not revealing too much emotion.

So I played an old song by the Everly Brothers called "Dream." Of course, Jorge and Ricardo did not understand a word of English. But that didn't seem to matter. They listened attentively. They smiled occasionally. They were extremely polite.

"Can we camp here?" Ricardo asked, pointing to their little wooden boat lodged on the sand but a few feet from my canoe.

"Of course," I said.

"Maybe you would want to visit our home tomorrow," Jorge said nodding, as if to mean that it was already agreed upon.

I smiled. "Yes, I would very much like to visit your home."

I was somewhat surprised that I had committed to it, since I tend to be a rather solitary man.

The brothers smiled back and made movements showing that they were ready to go to sleep. But I had one more question to ask.

"Did you build that boat?"

"Yes," Ricardo said.

"What tools did you use?"

The brothers glanced at each other.

"Unos machetes. Y martío. Y serrucho," Ricardo said.

They must have seen the look of surprise in my eyes because Jorge added, "We cut and shape the wood with our machetes. We use the saw to cut the wood into planks. From a big tree. Un palo que tiene mucho aceite. The oil keeps the water out."

"No nails?" I asked.

Ricardo chuckled. "Sometimes. But we can make a glue from another plant; it is really only to seal the seams. And we make wooden pegs to fasten the boat together. It takes about a month to make a boat. Sometimes more."

"How long will a boat like that last?" I asked.

Jorge made a wry face. "If you take care of a boat, then it will last a long time."

"That boat is—" Ricardo looked at the stars, his tongue coursing over his upper lip, "— three years old."

"No, it's older than that," Jorge said. "It's at least four years old."

"How long will that boat last?" I asked again.

"Ten years, easy," said Ricardo.

"There is a man from a village farther downriver from where we live who is very good at making boats," Jorge said. "He is an uncle of ours."

"Maybe someday I could meet him," I said.

"Sí, como no," Jorge replied.

I was still tired, the kind of exhaustion that isn't relieved by just one night's rest. I hoped that by tomorrow I would be feeling better.

Jorge and Ricardo walked back to their boat and turned it on its side and fashioned a crude bed underneath: two blankets on the sand. They seemed not the least worried about the snakes or insects that might be crawling on the narrow beach at night.

The fire was out. And from my tent I again looked up at the heavens. The moon was entering its first quarter. Juan's visits into distant galaxies would be less successful now that moonbeams were beginning to overpower starlight. I should be leaving in a few days, I thought.

Using the light from my flashlight, fresh batteries installed, I wrote in my journal for about thirty minutes before finally going to bed.

I had been thinking a lot about the logging I'd seen from the south side of the mountain. Juan and don Miguel had said that as much as half of the wood felled was burned on the spot and made into charcoal. I wondered if every time I bought a bag of charcoal and it read *Hecho en México*, or something to that effect, I was only adding to the carnage I'd witnessed from the mountain?

I recalled also Juan's comments about the people who were logging the forest's hardwoods. He'd said that the man in charge had obtained counterfeit land titles, something that is common in Mexico, and that this man had a history of such behavior. Juan had said that the tactic is quite simple: you muddy the real title by bribing an official and then you extract as much timber as you possibly can, all the while continuing to bribe officials to slow the process of clearing the title by the legitimate landowners. By the time the title is cleared, you've made a substantial profit and so you leave—in the dead of night sometimes—and begin operations somewhere else.

Perhaps the legitimate owners were too tired or overwhelmed to fight someone like the man who was logging the hardwoods? Decent and honest people wouldn't resort to the kind of tactics that some have employed in order to oust those who have entered to abuse the land. But then again, I'd seen, in both Mexico and the United States, "rightful owners" who had misused the land as badly as the loggers south of the mountain were now doing illegally.

I sat in my tent perplexed and saddened, that question about why we behave toward the earth the way we do still unresolved. Others much greater than I have grappled with the question. Aldo Leopold examined the "land ethic" long ago in his *Sand County Almanac* and was thus one of the first to bring attention to the topic.

About Leopold, Eric Freyfogle writes in *Justice and the Earth:*

> The solution—or at least part of the solution Leopold thought most important—was a new attitude toward the land within each person who controlled a portion of the Earth's resources. Conservation, [Leopold] believed, required a change of heart, a new orientation not based on economic self-interest. The issue was one of philosophy, not science or economics. (181)

Late that night I was awakened by a sound that was half roar and half cry. I sat up and looked out through the tent's mosquito mesh. I know Jorge and Ricardo heard the noise because one of them mumbled something to the other, though I don't believe either sat up for a look. It had been a tormented sound, but not the sound of animals fighting or of being attacked. Once in the mountains of New Mexico I was awakened by squeals and yelps and groans that made it sound as if the banshee herself had just ripped into the guts of some unsuspecting soul. My wife sat up next to me and we both poked flashlight beams out into the night. What's going on? she asked. Must be bears, I said. And then we saw two fat raccoons dart in front of our tent, each biting the other. Can you believe it? I asked Norma. She shook her head and said she didn't know they could make that much noise.

But the noise I heard here on this lonely beach was different. It had a wailing quality to it. As if it were a plea of some sort, and I was just too ignorant to understand it.

The Ninth Day

"You can go with us in our boat," Jorge said, after downing the last of his morning coffee.

I nodded and said, "Buen idea," still feeling tired from the two days on the mountain.

Ricardo stood, fiddling for a second with the frayed edges of his straw hat's brim. He placed the hat on his head and smiled. "My mother will fix you a tonic. It will help you feel better."

So we shoved off, though I felt a slight reluctance upon leaving the solitude of my river camp.

A corridor of trees and fuzzy-leafed herbs jutting out from the base of the mountain to the edge of the beach began obscuring the view of my tent and canoe. I sighed, a bit nervous about this unscheduled trip, and contemplating the juvenile who wanted to lean over the side of the tiny boat and drag his hands in the water and who labored to see past eyes wearing wire-rimmed trifocals.

"Este es un buen lugar para pescar," Jorge said, his right hand affixed to the rudder pole, his left hand holding a lemon slice I'd given him.

"Do you fish here often?" I asked.

"There are other good places. But we come here now and then."

"What kinds of meat besides fish do you eat?"

Jorge sucked hard on the lemon slice, made a face, grinned. "We have goats. Some chickens."

"How about deer meat?"

Jorge shrugged. "My older brother Carlos has a shotgun that an American gave him years ago. Carlos was a guide."

"What kind of guide?"

"Para las palomas y alas blancas."

"But he has no ammunition for his shotgun," Ricardo said, maintaining a gentle and quiet rhythm on the two oars.

"If Carlos had ammunition we would hunt deer," Jorge said.

"Are there many deer?" I asked.

"Sí muchos. Pero son muy pequeños." Jorge held his hand up about two and a half feet over the water to indicate their size.

"They are little, but they are very fast," Ricardo added.

We had reached a point where we could see the western flank of La Viuda. From this perspective she was draped in subtle shades of green, emerald to olive gray. Like a thousand woolly droplets tossed randomly against the mountain, the trees masked the rocky surface beneath. Near the summit, I saw two hawks, too far away to discern their color or markings. They dipped their wings left and right, gliding; from this distance, they seemed but a few feet from the mountainside.

I saw where another small basin worked its way up to about one third the mountain's height. Perhaps another melon rock wash divided that basin. But there seemed no shelves to camp on above it. From where the little basin began, a place shaped like an inverted nose, the mountain rose steeply, almost straight up.

I scanned the mountain with my binoculars. The trees grew so close together that I could glimpse only a few bald spots, tiny gravel-covered clearings.

A fish jumped a few feet from the boat. When I turned at the sound of its splash, I noticed Jorge staring at me.

"What are you thinking, my friend?" I asked.

He seemed shy and nervous, but finally said, "You have not told us what you do. In Texas. Where you live."

I nodded. "I am a writer." I was thinking that there are other things that I do, but writing is all that really matters.

"A writer?" Jorge raised his eyebrows and looked at his brother.

"What do you write about?" Ricardo asked.

As I was about to answer, I realized I did not have anything specific to say. If I said I wrote about a lot of things, then that would be meaningless. If I said I wrote about one thing, then that would be inaccurate. I thought to say that I wrote about life. But that seemed pretentious. *Maybe I should say I write about nature?* But that, too, sounded absurd, almost comical. *How does one write about nature?* By describing it? By communicating the feelings one has when within it? *Oh my, not to these fellows. What can I say that doesn't sound frivolous?*

"I write about the things I have experienced," I said.

"You have experienced many things?" Jorge asked.

"I have experienced a few things. Like any man. But for whatever reason there might be, I must write about those things."

The brothers were silent. I wondered what they were thinking.

Then Jorge said, "There are people who love to tell a good story."

"Because they can tell it well," Ricardo added, laughing.

I laughed too.

A male Mexican trogon—bright green back and head, dark red belly, distinctive white band along its breast—was standing on a limb of a tree with branches exploding in all directions from its base.

"Qué bonito," I said in a low voice.

"Yes," Jorge said, pointing at the bird with his chin. "There are many birds here."

Even as Jorge's words were fading, I wondered what the similarities were between my appreciation of nature and his. Most people, in my world, view nature merely as something that must be controlled or tamed. In some circles, we even believe that naked vistas—plowed fields, city parks, manicured landscapes—are desirable over real nature. Some people, in fact, have built a whole philosophy on the idea—even though there is no substantial proof to support it—that humans *prefer* naked vistas like parks and lawns. They claim, again with no tangible proof, that we bear an innate predilection for open areas because we evolved in places that were like that. But this is nothing more than hypothesis twisted into a claim of reality because it conforms to popular cultural dogma, and because those who have disseminated it are charismatics within their field.

So when those of us who disdain the acts of people who see no reason for nature—other than finding ways to profit from it— find birds and other animals living within uncontrived lands, like the land that bordered the river I was now boating, we are filled with concentrated emotions. Because pure lands are unnatural in our world. Even what my world considers pure lands are in reality contrived nature. For what is ecosystem management—in parks, refuges and sanctuaries—if not another form of development?

But here, along this placid river it was different. In Jorge's and Ricardo's world, at least for now, lands exist naturally, a harmonic circle completed within and around them. For me to say "What a beautiful bird" might be akin to their remarking, "That is a fancy billboard."

Yes, there are many billboards here . . . in my world.

"Do you know that people are cutting down the forest less than twenty kilometers from here?" I asked Jorge.

"A man who lives in a town that way—" Jorge pointed to the northeast "—has been cutting the trees for about a year."

"I was on the mountain, La Viuda, a couple of days ago. I could see that they are not far from here."

"How close?" Jorge asked.

"I think you will be able to see them in about a year, right here," I said.

Jorge did not speak.

"If they cut down all the timber then this land will change," I said.

"Yes," Jorge mumbled.

"You will not see the birds. Nor will there be any other animals."

Thirty minutes later we arrived at the place Jorge and Ricardo called home. We docked at the end of a narrow, well-worn trail that led up an embankment until it reached a flat area about a quarter acre in size.

A barking dog, outrageously large ears and sandy brown coat powdered liberally with black speckles, ran down the trail to greet us. I kept back until Ricardo petted it and spoke to it. The dog wagged its tail, approaching me with eyes begging forgiveness for whatever innocent intentions might have embarrassed its master.

"Hola perrito. Cómo estás perrito?"

We climbed the trail, the dog at my side, wiry tail whipping my legs.

There were two other dogs—a black and white one that appeared to be of mixed spaniel breed, and a gray female that seemed part whippet. But they held back, ears laid flat against their skulls and barking loudly. Then they too approached cautiously.

We entered a shadowy place. The sweet smell of burning wood and thin smoke huddling in pockets unseen but real as we walked in and out of them. Amidst a cluster of eight jacales, in four pairs, twig and mud walls packed within spaces created by coupled sticks planted vertically into a soft earth. Each kitchen jacale faced its bedroom jacale, the pairs linked by rickety porches from which hung strings of pink garlic and crimson pepper, green Aguila brand kerosene lanterns, and circles of strong, white Mexican rope. Underneath, propped against the mud and stick walls, were worn machetes and pitchforks, rusting shovels, rakes, pickaxes and hoes. With little tables handmade and chairs likewise. A communal oven made from hardened mud, with handmade brick lining its chamber's floor, stood beneath the bowed trunk of an ancient tree. Within the oven's dark portal sat three blackened Dutch ovens, each neatly inserted atop pulverized coals, their long spindle handles projecting outward. A reddish rooster and five yellow chickens walking and clucking. A wicker cage half the size of a bushel basket hung from the swooping limb of another tree; its little door swung permanently open, vacant within.

Two women in cotton dresses, one light blue, the other red, both long to mid-calf with white and yellow flowers embroidered over full bodices, watched me carefully.

I stood nervously, not realizing until that moment how accustomed I had become to my solitude.

An old man, walking upright and proud, emerged from the paired jacales on my right.

"This is my father," Jorge said.

We shook hands. His name was Salvador.

"And this is my mother." Jorge gestured at the old woman walking out from the kitchen jacale and wiping her hands on a black and white checkered apron.

More handshakes. She was doña Luce.

Six children, ranging in ages from about two to twelve, huddled around us. A little naked boy, brown and fat. A frail-looking girl, three maybe, with disheveled hair and an ugly scar on her right calf and wearing a print dress faded blue with little white flowers covering it. Another little girl, five or six, dark as the earth beneath her, huge black eyes and wavy black hair, and in a bright blue dress, the kind the Indians sell at the markets. And two boys of eight or nine, in worn jeans, shirtless, with smudged faces under prickly black hair. And the girl—the one I figured to be about twelve—tall and thin, her face the light brown color of the reed poles growing at the river's edge, her eyes honey-colored, her hair brown and stringy.

"These two are mine," Jorge said, smiling and pointing at the girl I guessed to be about twelve and at one of the shirtless boys.

"Hijito, véngase." Timidly, the other shirtless boy approached Ricardo. "Donde están tus hermanas?"

Don Salvador answered. "Your brother Samuel took Gloria and Mirna and Martín and Jesús to check on the goats."

"And the rest?" Ricardo asked.

"At the river." Don Salvador pointed farther downstream. "Carlos went to look for the donkey. San Juanita and José went with him."

We sat in a crude circle—on a couple of logs, on some handmade chairs, on a store-bought stool, on the ground—eating cabrito asado. Drinking fruit juice made from papaya and watermelon. With tortillas de masa and frijoles negros y arroz con chile. And hot pico de gallo. Don Salvador and doña Luce. Their four sons—Carlos, forty-one; Jorge, thirty-eight; Ricardo, thirty-five; Samuel, twenty-eight. The wives of the four sons: San Juanita, Rosalva, Patricia, and Lupita. And seven grandsons and five granddaughters.

"Yes, we have two sisters," Samuel said. "But they live with their husbands."

"Panchita lives in Victoria. She has two children," said doña Luce, a smile wrinkling her small dark face from forehead to chin.

"Tomasa lives in Reynosa," Samuel added.

Samuel's six-year-old daughter, Angélica—her bright blue Indian dress accenting her stark black eyes—sat next to me. When I'd first arrived, she announced: "Mira! El hombre tiene ojos verdes."

A minute later she was back, an entourage of cousins and her little naked brother behind her.

"Do you see differently from those green eyes?" she asked.

"Be quiet, that's not polite," said her mother, Lupita, staring and waiting for an answer.

"What color do you see this leaf?" I asked Angélica.

"Green," she said.

"Well it's green for me too."

Angélica's big eyes narrowed.

We all sat in the shade, facing one another, the smoldering coals from a small fire off to one side, the smell of cooked cabrito and burning wood hovering around us. The sounds of children's voices, adult conversation, dogs barking, the breeze fluttering the leaves, doves cooing in the forest. And laughter, of both children and adults. The reddish rooster working his way in and out of the gathering. A mother reprimanding her child for pushing a cousin. A dog walking up and grabbing one of the bones thrown to it. The green mountains surrounding us. Greasy fingers. Sated stomachs. A stack of hot tortillas replenished every few minutes.

"I was living in Reynosa with my sister and her husband," Samuel said. "I thought about going to the United States." He paused, shook his head. "I have friends who went to the United States. One lives in Houston now." A dour look. "But it is no good for me there. Everybody is crazy."

"In Reynosa or Houston?" I asked.

He smiled. But it was a cautious smile. "I was working in a maquiladora. So was my sister, Tomasa." Samuel glanced at his brother Carlos. "Tomasa's husband made her quit. And then I quit."

"Porqué?" I asked.

"Her husband started a business. He needed her help."

Samuel's eyes narrowed, and I could see the father-daughter resemblance in little Angélica.

"Why did *you* quit?" I asked.

Samuel shrugged. "There are not many jobs for men at the maquiladoras."

"But you quit anyway."

Though his face was dark, I could see an angry flush working its way across it. "My job was to load empty barrels on trucks. The barrels smelled like venom. They made me sick. I would go home and vomit. And I would get bad headaches."

"So it was better that you walked away," I said.

"Yes," Samuel scowled.

"Men must breathe," don Salvador said suddenly.

The sons all agreed, as if they had discussed this many times before. And as if they had come to some conclusion that they expected me to understand outright.

There was a moment of quiet. Then the women began to move about, picking up the tin and clay plates and asking if anyone wanted their clay cups refilled with juice. They shuffled the children off then went about the work of maintaining their homes.

As if on cue, the men stood, so I stood as well. Don Salvador walked slowly to the shade of a tree at least fifty feet high. The sons and I followed. El viejito sat. He was probably in his early seventies, five feet, six inches tall, más o menos, but his black hair had hardly any gray. The rest of us sat under the tree next to him. Ricardo's son brought a quart-sized clay jug and handed it to his father. The boy's sister brought six clay cups. Ricardo filled the cups from the jug, then handed each of us a cup.

I sniffed my cup when it was given me, thinking it might be pulque or some other fermented drink. But it was only more of the papaya and watermelon juice we had enjoyed earlier.

"El señor Longoria es escritor," Jorge said to his father.

"Ah, qué interesante." Don Salvador smiled and nodded.

I didn't feel like getting involved in another discussion on my writing, so I decided to ask a question.

"Do you own this land?"

Some hesitation, sideways glances.

"They say it belongs to a man who lives in Tampico, or Reynosa. But we have never met him," don Salvador replied.

"But he allows you to live on his land?" I said.

More sideways glances.

"We do not steal. We do not molest anything. Why can't we live here?" Samuel said, defiantly.

"In Mexico there have always been problems with who owns the land," Carlos said.

"They are fighting a war in the south over that right now," Samuel blurted.

"In Chiapas?" I asked.

"Yes, Chiapas." Samuel seemed impatient. "And maybe soon in other places."

Both Carlos and Ricardo started to say something, but don Salvador held his hand up. "In the cities many people are hungry. And others live like slaves on the big ranches. Even on the ejidos there are sometimes problems. The people steal from each other. And they fight among themselves."

"How do you know that?" I asked, contemplating the mass exodus across the border into the United States as a proclamation of that fact.

Don Salvador sighed. "Carlos was a soldier for nearly ten years. He saw many things. Bad things."

Carlos nodded ruefully. "En México los ricos y los políticos son los que controlan todo. Los pobres son nadamás perros flacos pediendo un pedasito de basura."

"Is it not that way everywhere?" I asked.

But no one said anything.

"This is a peaceful place to live," I said breaking the silence. "I would like to live here."

But something in that remark, judging from the lack of affirmation, did not sit well with the men.

"Well," I said, "I guess it's peaceful because there aren't too many people here."

This time the men agreed.

Don Salvador crossed his left arm over his stomach, his right elbow, wrinkled and bony, resting on the back of his left hand. He thought a moment, slowly kneading his chin with the fingers of his right hand. "I think," he finally said, "it is difficult to say why a place is peaceful."

For another long moment nothing more was said. The men sipped their fruit drinks. A couple of chickens scratched the ground nearby. A black vulture circled upward near a cerro that rose like a green pyramid a kilometer away. The leaves rustling in a steady breeze. The sounds of children playing.

Don Salvador extended his right hand outward. "In some places there are ranches that go for many kilometers." He paused, plucked a piece of grass, examining it as he spoke. "When I was a boy, we lived on a ranch that was over one hundred kilometers square. It was owned by one family. Many cattle. Many crops. We worked long hours. Like slaves. We could not plant one stalk of corn unless the owner of the ranch said we could. We could not kill a deer unless he gave us permission. We could not build anything unless he said it was possible. We could not go walking on our own unless he approved. We could not buy a horse and call it ours. Everything belonged, whether we realized it or not, to him."

"You *were* slaves," Samuel said firmly.

Don Salvador did not reply.

"What does it mean to own something?" I asked, knowing I might be stirring the pot once more.

Don Salvador considered the question. Then he said, "Tengo dos machetes buenos. Carlos tiene una escopeta. Está camisa, mis pantalones, mis zapatos son míos."

"Do you own the jacale you sleep and eat in?" I asked.

Don Salvador chuckled. "It is made of mud and sticks. The roof is like the grass I hold in my hand. It covers my head when it rains. It keeps me warm in the winter." He smiled. "There is a bird that built a

THE NINTH DAY

nest in the mud. I can show it to you if you want. And the wasps make their nests along the eaves."

"But you built it. Didn't you?"

Don Salvador was looking at his sons. Perhaps he had more to say to them than to me? He plucked another blade of grass. "I gathered mud. And picked up sticks that had fallen from the trees. I put them together. The wasps bring more mud and water to make their nests. And the bird brings more sticks."

"And someday it will all fall down," I said.

The old man laughed. He had a lump the size of a grape under his skin on the left side of his face, about an inch under his ear. When he laughed the lump moved freely, as if it was not attached to any muscle or bone. I guess he realized I was looking at it.

"Many years ago a thorn broke off in my face. I could not get it out. This ball grew over it," he said.

"Why didn't you go to a doctor to have it removed?"

Don Salvador shrugged. "It does not really bother me. And doctors sometimes do more harm than good. Besides, I think this ball is lucky."

"Cómo?" I asked.

"It tells me things. When north winds are coming. When rain is near."

Ricardo laughed. "People ask my father, 'What does your face tell you today, abuelo?'"

Don Salvador grinned, a right lower canine and premolar missing. "I am big," he said. "The bird is small. The wasps are even smaller." He noted the size of the birds and the wasps with his fingers. "I can put more mud and sticks together than either the birds or the wasps. But I have seen jacales that had hundreds of old wasps' nests along the eaves. I have seen where the birds have built up the walls by making many nests." He paused. "Do you think those birds and wasps have a part in owning the house? Did they not help make the whole what it is?"

"You have a point, abuelo," I said. "But your ideas are not shared by many people."

Don Salvador wrinkled his forehead. "What do you mean? Many people think the way I do."

But before I could answer, he added, "It is just that some people believe that only their thoughts are good. That all other ways of thinking are bad."

Doña Luce had walked over to where we were sitting. She said something to Jorge and Carlos about the donkey, and they got up and walked off. She stayed.

Don Salvador continued: "Last year a man came here in a boat. A very big boat. It had a big motor. It had big seats to sit on. The boat was red and silver. The man was from Texas." Don Salvador looked at doña Luce. "You remember him, don't you?"

She nodded. "Sí, como no. Yo me recuerdo."

"He and his guide camped by the river. All day long he would fish." Don Salvador raised his right hand, palm up. "But every fish he caught, he would throw back into the water. He would just hook the fish and then let them go."

"That is true," doña Luce said.

"What kind of a man would do that?" Don Salvador asked. "What kind of people think nothing of tempting the fish?"

"They call it 'catch and release,'" I answered. "That way the rivers won't be fished out. By releasing the fish someone else can come along to enjoy the fishing." I hesitated. "Do you think the hook is painful to the fish?"

"The pain comes not from the hook, but from the way the man thinks," don Salvador replied.

"Así son los Americanos," Samuel added, watching me, perhaps for a reaction.

But don Salvador gave me no chance to answer. "I think fishing was just a game for that man," he said looking at doña Luce. She agreed.

"He did not eat the fish," the old man continued. "He only taunted them. The fish was something by which he entertained himself. No animal should be treated that way."

I nodded. "But we ate the goat."

"Yes, the goat gave its life so we can live."

"And someday we give our lives so the worms can live?"

The old man made a face. "We hunt and fish. We take only what we need. We return what we take from the earth when we die. It is a cycle, and it must be allowed to live."

"Live?" I asked.

Don Salvador nodded. "The man who came here with the big boat said he threw the fish back into the water because he wanted it to live. So I asked him: 'If you want it to live, then why do you abuse it so?' But he did not understand. He laughed and said, 'Fish have no feelings.'"

"Did you reply?" I asked.

"Yes. I told the man, '*You* are the one who has no feelings.'"

"What did he say when you said that?"

Don Salvador grinned. "He did not say anything to me after that. The next day the man and his guide left. I heard they fished farther down river for almost a week. But I think he thought we were backward. That we were not smart enough to think like him. I think he thought of himself as better than we."

"What do you think about that?" I asked.

The old man looked away, a faint smile. "We think differently, of that I am sure. But I do not think that he is better than me." He paused, looking down at the grass in front of him. "In truth, I felt sorry for him. He will live his life and never have understood it."

Doña Luce nodded, hands cupped in her lap. "Everything is a toy for people like that."

"Only God has the right to play with living things," don Salvador said.

I nodded thinking, *Yes, but have we not become gods?*

That afternoon I walked with Jorge and Carlos and four of the children to the river. I was sleepy from the heavy meal and I wished I could lie down and take a nap. They had each brought a bucket to fill with water; I took a bucket as well. We dipped the buckets in the river, but did not immediately return them to the settlement. Instead, we sat, and as the children waded and played in shallow water, we talked.

Almost immediately I felt a gap between us. I wanted to talk about the land and about the birds of the area; I wanted to discuss their feelings about the logging on the other side of the cerros; I wanted to find out what their thoughts and sentiments were about Mexico's politics. But neither brother seemed inclined to speak on any of those things.

They knew about a few birds. After some description, they both said they knew the tinamou. "It is like a little, brown chicken," Jorge said.

I told them that I had first visited the general area in the late 1970s and had made several subsequent trips since then. I said that on my first trip to this dry forest region, I had heard the whistle calls of hundreds of tinamous every day. Now I heard only a few.

Jorge and Carlos nodded and seemed to be contemplating my statement; but neither, at least outwardly, appeared to draw any conclusions from my observations.

They knew a few other birds: the parrots and parakeets, the owls, hawks and vultures, motmots and brown jays, and some of the woodpeckers. But there were no serious distinctions made between different species in any one group. An owl was an owl, although they said that in the forest lived big owls and little owls, and that most owls brought bad luck.

"If you see one owl then you hope to see another owl because the second owl will nullify the bad luck of the first," Carlos said.

"Are you crazy?" Jorge scolded. "That's not the way it works. If you see two owls then your bad luck is compounded."

"I like seeing owls," I said—but realizing I'd just increased the gap.

Carlos stood when he saw a turtle climbing a muddy branch that leaned out of the water about fifty yards away.

"Those are good to eat," he said. But at that instant the turtle dropped back into the water. Survival of the fittest, I thought.

After a moment of quiet I turned to Jorge and said, "I think you and Ricardo heard that roar last night that seemed to have a wailing quality to it."

"Yes, we heard it," he replied. "It was a tigre walking along that little canyon near where we were camped."

I realized he was talking about the melon wash I had scaled up the mountain. And I remembered the large cat track I'd seen near the tiny watering hole at my spike camp, and the large dropping as well.

Carlos raised both hands. "You never see los tigres. But their scat is everywhere."

"Ricardo saw one," Jorge blurted. "He was walking in the monte and he saw a tigre from here to there." Jorge pointed at the children about twenty feet away.

"I'd sure like to see a jaguar," I said. And again the gap widened.

I had brought along a blue nylon pup tent. I set it under the tall tree where we had sat and talked after eating dinner.

No one ate supper. I don't think it was because of a lack of food. It's just not their habit. They were not skinny, but sinewy. I would imagine, discounting a few intestinal parasites, that they are probably healthier than most Americans. Of course, I'm considering overall health: mental, spiritual, physical. Besides, what we lack in parasites we make up for in heart disease. And anxiety and depression. Some, I'm sure, will construe such statements as nothing more than senseless romanticism. But that is a sentiment based on the pride of the uninformed. Spend a few days with these people and you will see how much simpler (and happier) their lives are.

At least some of our differences, I'm sure, have to do with upbringing. My father is a businessman and inventor of sorts, and my mother is a pianist and singer. Both my parents, though not avid outdoors people, have always had special feelings about the land. But my father would not be content with the daily labor of carrying the water buckets from the river to the settlement. He would have devised some mechanical means to channel the water from the river. He would have looked at the way the jacales were built and then said: You know, I can make it better. He would have done those things because he is a person who enjoys the mental exercise of invention as much as he despises having to do manual labor.

I too was thinking about better ways of bringing the water, both for human consumption and for irrigation, from the river to the settlement. And I was thinking also about my curiosity with respect to the birds and other animals and plants. And then I thought about that inquisitiveness and the way it often spawns enterprises. I thought how some people might consider that resourcefulness good, and how others would suggest that it has given us problems as well. Perhaps it all has to do with the extent to which we apply our resourcefulness, and with the way we think of ourselves in the process. The word *autodiocentric* came to mind. And so did the words *obligation* and *virtue*—especially when referring to the land. In *A Sand County Almanac,* Aldo Leopold wrote:

> The existence of obligations over and above self-interest is taken for granted in such rural community enterprises as the betterment of roads, schools, churches, and baseball teams. [The] existence [of obligations] is not taken for granted, nor as yet seriously discussed, in bettering the behavior of the water that falls on the land, or in the preserving of the beauty of diversity of the farm landscape. Land-use ethics are still governed by economic self interest. (245)

I wonder what Leopold would have thought about my contemplating easier ways to channel water from the river to the settlement? Perhaps he would have said: "It's a good idea as long as you balance those efforts with the needs of the land and its other inhabitants." But I know Leopold was skeptical about motives. He also wrote:

> When the private landowner is asked to perform some unprofitable act for the good of the [natural] community, he today assents only with outstretched palm. If the act costs him cash this is fair and proper, but when it costs only fore-thought, open-mindedness, or time, the issue is at least debatable. (250)

The night came behind shadows spawned by the clustering of cerros: rounded mounds and spiked peaks and diminished flats. At dusk, the sun skipped reddish planks across a sojourn of sundry clouds, holding in that instant a sodality of water fragmented, each traveler but a great bird homeward bound, the carrier of what parts begin the whole anew. Soon afterward the people secluded themselves in their jacales. Children's voices hushed by sleep; the smell of burning wood dissolved by the fragrances of living plants; the night's quiet punctuated by calls from nocturnal birds, and fish jumping in the river but a few yards away. All the while my thoughts worming amidst twigs and loose earth, finding places to settle and look about.

The Tenth Day

The trail wove secretively through shrubs and saplings, leviathan and bantam leaved, the lot adorned with numberless diamonds, that ephemeral remnant of a heavy morning dew; and amidst greater trees twisting and climbing lazily into a clear blue heaven—from which fell a white light subdued quickly into a scattering of photon feathers, gold and silver, each alighting without fanfare atop a black earth. From the canopy echoed the calls of untold birds, our glimpses of them confined to blues, reds, and yellows that appeared briefly against a curtain of green.

"Está lejos la cueva?" I whispered.

"No," Jorge said. "It is in the rocks at the base of the cerro that looks like a pyramid."

A gentle tap on my shoulder. "Los tigres duermen en esas cuevas," Carlos said.

"Sí," Jorge agreed, pointing his black machete in the direction of the cave.

"You hunt the jaguar?" I asked.

"No," Samuel said adamantly, walking behind me and alongside Carlos. "We do not eat *cats.*"

"But I hear you have a shotgun."

"La escopeta es mía," Carlos said. "Pero no tengo parque."

"Es una doce. Doble cañones," Samuel added.

Carlos picked a caterpillar off his shirt sleeve, then laid it on the long leaf of a vine. "Guns are illegal in Mexico." He smiled cynically. "It is nearly impossible to find ammunition. Unless you have a special permit. Unless you belong to a shooting club."

"But Mexico is still an armed camp," I said.

Carlos nodded. "But guns are mostly in the hands of the military. And the police. And the rich."

"If the poor had guns then all the animals would be quickly killed off," I said.

Carlos did not reply.

"You do see what I mean. Don't you?"

"That is possible," Carlos said. "But the rich kill many animals also. I saw it when I was a guide. The rich Americans and Mexicans would kill thousands of white-winged doves. In just one day. And they would leave them to rot in the fields."

"Where did you guide?" I asked.

"Near the town of San Fernando."

"Whoever has the guns, has the power," Samuel said.

I smiled. "It is that way everywhere, my friend. But if *you* had the power, are you certain you would not abuse it?"

I could tell that Samuel had mixed feelings about me. Early that morning he and I had sat next to his jacale talking. Of the four brothers, he was the most handsome: straight thin nose, large black eyes, wavy brown hair, thin muscular build, five nine, maybe a half inch more. But he was also the most impetuous. We talked about overpopulation. And about politics. And about the logging I had seen to the south.

"Have you noticed that smoky haze that comes when it hasn't rained?" I'd asked him. I did not know it at the time, but that same haze was already moving northward and would eventually cover all of Texas and the entire midwestern United States and even reach into Canada.

Samuel frowned. "Oh yes. We all see it. It is from the D.F. And from Veracruz. And south to the border."

"Maybe it's because there are too many people in the Distrito Federal. In all of Mexico, actually. The land cannot support so many people."

But Samuel had other reasons. He said the haze came from los impresarios ricos. It was residue from the imperialist's machine. The masses were just victims.

There was probably some truth in what he said. He did not know however, nor did I, that most of the haze was coming from grass and brush fires set by peasant farmers employing traditional slash and burn agricultural methods.

"The poor in Mexico have always been abused by those in power— the extreme Right mainly," Samuel added.

I did not reply. But in my guts I knew that if Samuel ever had the power, he would be as wasteful and greedy and exploitative as those he hated. I did not tell him that the Right uses things and people suffer. And the Left uses people and things suffer. There is no other real difference between them. I decided, instead, to tread softly around Samuel. He was schooled and he was angry. Of the brothers, he seemed the least aware of this place. He was perhaps as much a foreigner here in this forest as was the fisherman from Texas who had come in his big red and silver boat.

But of the other brothers, I was unsure. If they had more luxuries, would they live "like Americans?" It was hard to tell. Maybe they would. Maybe they would not. Quite possibly that was why don Salvador seemed to speak more to his sons when speaking to me. Maybe he wanted to make sure they would see what he saw. Or what he knew. That in this world things change now all too fast, and what you had often disappears without leaving a trace, but for the memories clutched to your heart. For now, don Salvador had found this place to live quietly, though I sensed that he was not completely happy even here. Perhaps he was one of those people Juan and don Miguel had said were hiding from the law. If he was, then he hid his past crimes well. But I do not know. He seemed like an old and gentle man. I think he just wanted to live in peace. Like another old man I used to know a long time ago, he probably knew that things were not ever going to get better until they got much worse. So bad that there was no choice but to go up. A long and arduous way upward. To some place that looked a lot like this. And if there were people about, then it would be like this too. Just a few people. Not enough to do much harm. Nor with the will or the way, or even the need to do harm. Most needs are unreal anyway. Material needs. Knowing needs. It seems that every time we seek to fill those "needs," something gets destroyed. Close by or far away. Sometimes both.

"We will have to cut through the monte here," Jorge said. He began hacking a shoulder-wide trail through vines and saplings, the sweat oozing profusely from his skin and soaking the faded red shirt he was wearing and forming a wet belt around the tops of his worn, light blue polyester pants. I wondered if his clothing, and that of his brothers and family, had been purchased new or used. Either way, I wondered how they obtained the money to buy anything from the world beyond this place.

In the Lower Río Grande Valley of Texas where I live, there are many warehouses stocking tons of used clothing. The Mexicans cross the border and spend long hours rummaging through the high piles, sorting out shirts, pants, sweaters, jackets, and dresses into cardboard boxes and plastic sacks. Sometimes they find shallow places along the Río Grande to walk the clothing into Mexico like human pack trains. More often, they simply bribe a Mexican Customs inspector, then drive inland where they sell the used clothes in tiny stores within obscure hamlets dotting the countryside—the arteriole tips of commerce and industry. The clothes are worn proudly by the poor, as well they should be. The refuse of the intemperate finds a longer-lived home in jungles and deserts and alongside mountains.

"Are there pinolíos here?" I asked.

"No," Jorge said. "Pinolíos are just along the river."

Carlos walked ahead, machete in hand, and joined Jorge in cutting the trail.

Abruptly, Jorge stopped.

"Mira!" He pointed to a large seed-filled dropping at his feet, round as a fifty-cent piece and nearly as long as a two-celled flashlight. This was neither mountain lion nor jaguar scat, no tubular matting of hairs from rabbit or javelina.

"The seeds in this dropping are from that plant," Jorge said, indicating an oblong fruit hanging from a small tree unfamiliar to me.

"Yo he visto excrementos de animales como ese en otras partes," I said, stooping to examine the dropping. "In the mountains of New Mexico. And in Colorado and Montana," I added.

"Es un oso," Jorge said.

I nodded. "Maybe. It *does* look somewhat like bear scat. But I've never heard of bears living around here, especially at this altitude."

Carlos flipped the scat over with his machete. Small white grubs were busy boring holes into the dropping's underside.

"My father says he saw a bear running away from the river once," Carlos said. "But he has never seen one since."

I picked the dropping up, rock hard, odorless. And finding it difficult to contain the feeling of the moment. *Just imagine, there might actually be bears here . . .* The kid wanted to dance, but the old man made sure the boy remained civil; the eyes of both traced the ground near the dropping, looking for tracks. There were none.

We found more scat about a hundred yards farther down the trail.

But again I found no tracks. All the while I wondered, *Can this really be a bear?* I imagine, however, that the scat actually came from a large coati. And quite possibly what don Salvador thought was a bear was really a male coati ambling to the river.

Carlos held his hand just below waist level. "The bears are small, only about this big."

"Anyone else seen them?" I asked.

"Some people see them, now and then," said Carlos.

"The bears are the most secretive animals here," Jorge said.

The cave was about six feet high and twelve feet across at its entrance, narrowing quickly less than fifteen feet from its mouth. The hole leading into the deeper parts of the cave was only about two feet in diameter. When we peered through the smaller opening I thought about histoplasmosis, the fungal disease often acquired by entering windless caves. I'd known a few people who came down with the fever, cough and malaise. The primary acute form is not too bad. I'd had worse with a bout of typhus and relapsing fever. But there was also the progressive disseminated form with bloody lungs, swollen liver and spleen, and gaping holes worn through the gut. And the chronic form that looks and acts a lot like tuberculosis.

"We can go in a little way," Carlos said, chipping off a small piece of the rock that covered the smaller hole.

I peeked inside. "Have you been in there?"

Carlos nodded. "It opens into a room just big enough to stand in. It goes back, then up, then down."

"How far down?"

"I have only gone back about fifty meters. It gets very cramped. It breaks into three tunnels." Carlos opened his hands to less than two feet.

"Hmm, that's pretty narrow."

"A man can crawl through. But you have to back out feet first," he said.

Again, I looked into the dark hole. Shook my head. "I don't think so." Shrugged. "Who knows." Stood up and stretched my back. "Maybe the cave does go many kilometers."

On our way back, Carlos cut vines like I had done that day on the mountain for the water they contained. We all did likewise. The water was cool and well filtered. We stopped and ate some of the bright red, golf-ball-sized fruit from a pitahaya cactus. The fruit's pulp is blood red with abundant little black seeds; it tastes sweet and juicy. I asked the brothers if they ate any of the other cacti growing along the hillsides.

"We've made candy from the biznaga," Jorge said. (*Biznaga* is a generic term for any of a number of squat barrel cacti growing from the southwestern United States into southern Mexico. I should add that the name *pitahaya* is also a generic term for several species of columnar cacti; the one we ate is known scientifically as *Acanthocereus pentagonus*.)

"How about the big organ cactus?" I asked, pointing to a species growing on the side of a nearby hill.

"No," Jorge and Carlos said.

"But some people eat it," Jorge added.

We kept walking, but stopped again when Jorge cut a small sapling and told me he was going to make a bow for his son.

"Does this wood make good bows?" I asked.

"Sí, es muy bueno. Muy flexible, pero también muy fuerte."

"So you hunt with a bow?"

"No, es para los niños nadamás."

We walked on. Slowly. Quietly. Until we reached a small clearing where a donkey with a light gray coat and black mane was grazing placidly about thirty yards away.

"How did *he* get loose?" Jorge said.

Carlos shrugged. "The boys probably didn't tie him right." He looked at me. "Stay here. We'll be right back."

While the three brothers tended to the donkey, I found shade under a tree and sat.

I've wondered about the ideas we have regarding academic studies of the environment: the discourses over ecology, conservation biology, toxicology, and other related fields. Those are worthwhile endeavors, but still I've questioned if the knowledge of how energy is transferred in nature or of how a species is being destroyed *really* makes us change our behavior? I've contemplated also the irony in creating careers like Environmental Science and Environmental Technology, which are dependent on a society continuing to pollute and desecrate the earth. But then Neil Evernden suggests in *The Natural Alien* that one must be watchful for how our environmental dilemma is defined:

I am fearful of the hypocrisy inherent in calling for a different approach and then falling into the usual pattern of thinking exclusively in terms of "problems" and "solutions." Or perhaps I should say in terms of "issues" and "solutions." (xi)

In referring to the book *Arctic Oil* by John Livingston, Evernden warns about the dangers in viewing our environmental difficulties as merely a series of overt physical events:

> [Livingston] suggests that the environmental dilemma, as reflected in the daily newspaper headlines, is commonly perceived as a series of issues—oil spills, endangered species, ozone depletion, and so forth—and that we are so overwhelmed by these that we seldom look deeper. (xi)

Over and over again, Evernden emphasizes that the true environmental crisis is of mind and not of biological ecology. Our predicament stems from the way we think and the behaviors that ensue from those thoughts.

David Noble has shown us that part of our thinking arises from the belief that by buttressing our faith with good works—science and technology—we can hasten our return to perfection. But there must have been other critical events that both preceded and followed Joachim of Fiore's perspicacious insight, that historical epiphany from which our culture drew its very direction and thus, perhaps, sealed its fate?

Maybe we should examine the idea of technology. Is technology, in and of itself, a bad thing? Or is the evil perceived to exist within it in fact revealed not in the tools we use but in the way we view ourselves when we use those tools?

Carlos and Samuel approached the donkey carefully while Jorge walked up behind it and grabbed the rope it was dragging. With the donkey now secured to a stout tree trunk, the brothers returned and sat with me in the shade.

"Have you ever heard of the people they say lived around that mountain called La Viuda—where I have my camp? They called them the Earth People?" I asked.

Carlos thought for a moment. Shook his head. "They were Indians, you say?"

"I have heard of them," Samuel said. "A man said they were all wiped out by soldiers many years ago."

"When?" Carlos asked.

"Long ago," Samuel repeated, annoyed.

"There are many stories," I said.

"But it is true," Samuel insisted.

"What else did you hear?" I asked.

"That they were very shy. They lived in caves. They had no use for clothing. They shaved their hair. Even the hair on their pubic regions."

"The man told you that?" I asked.

"Some of it. I have heard things about them from other people too."

"What other things?"

"That they spoke a strange tongue. And they hunted with bows." Samuel waved his hand at the cerros. "All around here."

"But why did the soldiers kill them?" I asked.

Samuel had a small stick in his mouth. He spat it out with a jolt. He was going to say something, but for some reason, he held back.

Carlos spoke instead. "The soldiers kill. The bandits kill. The police kill. *Todos matan.*"

Again, it looked as if Samuel wanted to say something, but he kept quiet. And I did not ask what might be on his mind.

We all stood and then ambled off the established trail to a creek that flowed out of the pyramid cerro. Narrow and rock bottomed, the creek plummeted rapidly into the great river a half kilometer away, its water glassy clear and frosty cool. I sat, watching both Carlos and Jorge cut wooden spears with their machetes.

"This is where there are some good fish," Jorge said.

At that moment a flock of yellow-headed parrots burst over us, cackling loudly and finding perches in the trees alongside the creek. Instantly, from those shredded associations cataloged haphazardly within the subconscious, I remembered eight bobwhite quail my son Jason and I had watched crash into a game-proof fence some months before in South Texas. The quail had flushed in front of my pickup as we drove a dirt road in Zapata County. Three of the birds were killed outright. Two more had broken wings. The rest flew off, disoriented.

"Are there any fences around here?" I asked.

"None close by," Carlos said.

Jorge had finished his spear. He stepped carefully from rock to rock, the spear held loosely in his right hand, his right arm cocked back, the spear's shaft nudged close to his ear.

"Why did you ask about fences?" Samuel asked.

"I guess I was just thinking about some great high fences that line the roads in some parts of Texas," I said.

"High fences?" Samuel repeated.

I pointed to the trees that the parrots had flown into; even as I spoke the birds were cackling and screeching above us.

"See that branch sticking out on that second tree?" I said, indicating a straight limb about ten feet from the tree's base.

"Sí," Carlos said.

"Well, the fences are about that high. And they're not made of barbed wire. It's more like chicken wire, except the wire is much thicker and stronger."

"What cattle do they have in Texas that require those kinds of fences?" Carlos asked, his spear now finished. He stood and balanced it in his right arm.

"They build those fences to trap the deer," I said.

Carlos walked off to try out his spear, and Samuel muttered, "Trap the deer?"

"Yes," I said. "I was driving once from Encinal to Freer. I saw a caracara swoop into the road to pick up a piece of carrion. It was a rabbit that had been struck by a car. A truck was approaching from the other direction. The caracara flew off to avoid being hit. But it collided with a high fence that lined the road. I stopped and reversed my pickup to examine the bird. Its wing was broken. But I couldn't catch it."

Carlos stood like a statue at the water's edge. His wooden spear held closely to his ear, his eyes steady on the creek. Suddenly, his arm catapulted downward, the spear but a long streak cutting transparent water, then bobbing up like a cork under a spray of cool droplets. A fish jumped. Carlos braced himself against the rocks and dipped his bare feet into the water. He grabbed the spear with his right hand. And grinned broadly as he climbed back atop the rocks to become a statue once again.

"Are there many fences like that in Texas?" Samuel asked, the only one now paying attention.

"Yes. Everywhere."

Jorge had walked farther upstream. He flung his spear at a fish, but missed.

"Those fences sound to me like giant walls," Samuel said.

"I guess so," I replied.

"And they're for the deer?" Samuel asked again.

I nodded. "You see in Texas hunting is big business. The deer are strictly managed on the bigger ranches. But I wonder who watches out for the small animals like raccoons, skunks, coyotes, javelina, and bobcats that are enclosed within those fenced-in properties? I would think that those big fences sometimes keep many smaller animals from breeding elsewhere."

"It sounds like a big zoo," Samuel said.

I smiled. "Yes, I guess so."

And for some reason I thought about the man from Texas who had come to fish in his big red and silver boat.

Carlos threw his spear again. Another miss. He stepped into the water, grabbed the stick, and then sat next to us. Breathing hard and wet from the waist down, he laughed and said, "When we were children we could spear a fish easily."

Jorge walked up holding a three-pound fish speared just behind the dorsal fin. I think he was disappointed because none of us had seen his achievement.

"You reached in and grabbed the fish. Then you speared it," Carlos said, laughing.

Jorge grinned. "Estás loco. That is what you would have to do. I speared him with one great shot."

When we got back to the family settlement there were five men— scruffy-looking types in their late twenties, early thirties—standing under the big tree where don Salvador and his sons and I had sat and talked the day before, and where I had set my pup tent during the night. Ricardo was with them. He smiled. But the men eyed me suspiciously.

"Family?" I asked Jorge.

"No," he said. "Parrot trappers."

Jorge and Carlos walked to where the men stood and began talking to them. Samuel and I sat on a handmade bench in front of his jacale.

"They intend to trap here?" I asked.

Samuel looked bored. "They have been here before. A year ago maybe. They trap all around here."

"And you and your family do not object?"

"What can we tell them?"

"What do you think about what they do?"

"Nothing. That is their work."

"Yes, I know. That is their work because there are people in places far away who will buy the parrots."

Samuel shrugged, disinterested.

"But do you know that for every parrot that makes it to the border, twenty or more die?"

"Tell that to the Americanos."

"I've run into hundreds of parrot trappers over the years. I know how they work. They put glue on a board that has grain spread over it. When parrots and other birds light on the boards they get stuck. Or they'll use snares or another parrot that's tied down like a decoy to bring in the wild birds. The trappers grab the birds, toss them into sacks. Most of the time the birds' skin peels off their feet and stays attached to the glue, or the snares cut their legs. Infection sets in. Most of the birds die."

"I don't think it would be a good idea for you to tell those men anything."

"No, I guess not."

"You see that fellow smoking the cigarette?"

I glanced at the man Samuel had indicated with his chin. Though his complexion was brown overall, there were shades of red and even black blended into his skin. He had a burly nose, from which a frenetic, jet black mustache seemed to grow; and he had pronounced cheek bones. His charcoal-colored hair was amply doused with hair tonic; it looked like shiny rubber. Wearing a sweat-smeared blue and brown striped flannel shirt, faded blue jeans, and black tennis shoes, he had not taken his eyes off me.

"They say he escaped from prison," Samuel said. "He lives near the ejido west of here. Those men know you are not from here."

We ate beans and corn tortillas with chile. Jorge shared his fish. Ricardo had caught six more at the river while tending the goats. We ate those fish as well. But this time only the men sat to eat. The women and children had either eaten earlier or would eat later. I did not ask.

Don Salvador, whom I had not seen until just before we gathered to eat, emerged from his jacale. I was not sure why he had not come out until now. He did not seem to be upset or ill. I did notice, however, that he never addressed the trappers directly.

I had walked into doña Luce's kitchen a few minutes before. Dark as night, save for cracks of sunlight coming through the door and through a small hole someone had drilled into the wall to the left of the fireplace, it owned the odors of hundreds of cooked meals. It smelled of chile and beans. And of onions and garlic hanging from its crossbeams. And cabrito asado and arroz con pollo. But it was not as hot inside the little room as I had expected it to be. The walls of mud and sticks were ten inches thick; the thatched roof was at least half that. It seems the sun's heat fares poorly against mud and grass. Only when I approached the small pot-bellied earth oven half-buried in the back wall did I feel any heat. But the warmth was dry. The rush of cool air when I exited felt like a sudden bath of cold water.

"Did you see the cave?" don Salvador asked me.

"Yes, but we did not enter it."

He smiled. "I too like the sun."

All the while, the leader of the parrot trappers kept an eye on me.

"Your name?" I asked him suddenly.

For an instant, he looked surprised. But just as quickly, he regained that vile composure I was finding abhorrent.

"Why do you want to know?" he said coldly.

"Because you seem interested in who I am."

"I know who you are."

"So tell me, who are you?"

He ignored me, dipping a tortilla into his bowl of beans and chewing it sullenly.

I began talking to no one in particular. "I know of places not too far north where the sounds of parrots and many other birds are no longer heard in the forests. Because the forests are all gone or because the birds have all been trapped out."

No one spoke.

"I know there is a market for parrots. Every month the customs officers in the United States seize dozens of them at the ports of entry. But I wonder why any man would rape his own land by taking away the birds so that people in another land can hear their songs?"

"Por el dinero."

Subdued laughter rose from some of the men.

It was the one I had mentally named Fat Trapper who had spoken. Less Indian than his partners; black stubble lined his unctuous jowls and gelatinous double chin. When he laughed the fat wiggled in waves down to his chest and bounced along his midline.

"*Ah,* for the money," I repeated.

"Yes," the fat trapper said, laughing again.

"It is the way of the world," I said.

We did not speak much after that. After the meal I asked Jorge if he would take me back to my camp. Before I left I gave don Salvador my pocket knife. I gave Carlos a small compass I had never used. I gave Ricardo a wire saw that was still in its plastic wrap unopened. And as I climbed into the wooden boat, I handed Samuel, who had walked down to the water's edge to push Jorge and me off, a book of the birds of Mexico. I had found it packed with my pup tent, an old Irby Davis field guide I had thought long lost.

"These are the birds that those men will trap and kill," I told him. "Regardless of who is to blame, these are the birds that will be no more when human populations grow beyond their farthest limits. The cities, and the farms that feed the cities, will consume the forests. And the birds and everything else that lives within these forests will be gone forever."

Samuel said nothing, but looked directly at me without blinking.

"If you really care about the people, then you must care about the earth first," I told him. "Without a healthy earth, there can be no healthy people."

Samuel seemed to smile, with his eyes at least. Then he pointed to the northeast, his face looking suddenly childlike. "Did you know that Fidel Castro lived on a ranch over that way when he was a young man?" he said.

"Castro?" I repeated, pretending ignorance, though I'd heard the story before.

"Yes. He came here with a friend. The friend's father owned the ranch."

"How long was he here?" A legitimate question since the people who had told me the story did not know how long Castro had stayed.

Samuel shrugged. "Maybe a year or more."

For a moment I did not know what to say. I wondered why Samuel had felt it important to tell me what he did. I was uncertain if he had heard anything I had said about the earth.

But as if purposely to break my silence, Samuel reached out and touched my left forearm. "The friend, the man whose father owned the ranch, went back to Cuba with Castro," he said.

"He left his father?" I asked.

Samuel nodded indifferently.

I worked the rudder as Jorge rowed the boat upriver. Behind us, to the west and about twenty kilometers away, began a series of ejidos, each with a population of about two to four hundred. In Mexico that would be called a sparse population. To the north the people jam into the cities along the frontera, and sprawl across the "rural" lands like so many ants, leafcutters and harvesters, demanding more space, more acreage, more food. It is the same to the west and south. Population pressure has created its usual problems. The people set the forests ablaze in order to clear land for farming. But everything, the animals and plants, must perish in the process. The frail farms that emerge can only be a transient antidote to a human mass that must have more and more and more. And still, the population grows.

Mexico's president proclaimed recently that crime is rampant across the land. The black market for guns has reached an all-time high. In Mexico most of the guns are in the hands of the government and the criminals; sometimes it's hard to tell which is which. Not unlike los Estados Unidos, I might add. Often the people in the cities and outlying areas are incapable of defending themselves from raids by both bandits and military. So they look now for guns, any kind of gun to defend themselves.

I did not bother to watch the shore moving past me. The black mood had walked in, and I could not bear to see anything that might be gone tomorrow.

"I told those men you were leaving your camp as soon as I took you there," Jorge said.

I nodded.

"If they knew you were going to be here, they might come to rob you."

When we reached the camp I gave Jorge my Canadian-made machete. He checked its balance. Proclaimed it to be good.

"I do not believe that you will trap the parrots," I told him.

Jorge smiled innocently. "There are many of them and few of us," he said.

I wondered if he meant there are many people like the parrot trappers and few people like us. Or whether he meant there are many parrots and few people. But I did not see any point in asking him. Jorge turned and waved. In less than five minutes he was rounding the bend and out of sight.

I surveyed the camp. It appeared unmolested.

Inside my tent lay the shotgun as I had left it under the sleeping bag. The Dutch oven sat next to the grill, a fine layer of sand coating its lid. My aluminum folding chair, lying beside the tent, had likewise gathered a lilliputian sand dune against it.

I grabbed my binoculars from my pack and looked north toward the escarpment where Juan was surely waiting and wondering. This was the end of my eighth day at the mountain. I had told him that I would be gone no more than ten days. He had said the stars would be good for about a week, after that he would have too much moonlight for a good viewing of the galaxies.

Before leaving with Jorge and Ricardo I had written a note saying that I would be visiting a small settlement to the west, just in case Juan decided to look for me. The note was untouched. Juan was showing his usual extreme patience, the forbearance and tenacity of one who spends long hours searching for shimmering dots through a tiny hole—light forms so minute and distant that they require the sensitivities of peripheral vision to be properly explored.

I weighed what Jorge had told me about the parrot trappers as I removed the flare from the shotgun's bore and replaced it with double-ought buck—the words *por el dinero* still audible in my mind.

I thought, too, of the leader of the parrot trappers, the whites of his eyes pigmented with incompatible emulsions from which an anger seemingly unreserved sprang forth. It would not be wise to tell him that all things finite cannot be made otherwise. Though that truth will not reduce itself because there are those who will not tolerate its fact.

After the sun's light had sought other places, I sat in the darkness strumming my guitar softly, the shotgun leaning against the back of my chair. At this very moment, I thought, there are people rushing down expressways in all the major cities of the world. And right now a baby was just born. And someone just died. And couples are making love. And people are watching television. And nightclubs are packed. And wars are raging.

And hospitals are full. And a few kilometers north of here don Miguel and doña María live. And to the west Jorge and his brothers and their wives and children, and don Salvador and doña Luce live too. And far away my family is going about their lives. And within a few meters the termites are busy working under the fallen logs. And in the river a fish is about to jump. And on the mountain the jaguar is drinking from the rocky pool. And I am here.

The Eleventh Day

In South Texas there lives a thorny shrub that sometimes grows into a small tree that carries the folkname *junco* (pronounced "hoonko"). Biologists call the plant *Koeberlinia spinosa*. A few years ago I spent a spring and summer observing junco because when it flowers, it smells of rotting flesh. I had first noticed the odor many years before while roaming the brush. When I followed the smell into the monte searching for carrion, I discovered hundreds of flies buzzing around a dark green madness of thorns with small white flowers pegged along the outer edges of stems that themselves ended in needle-sharp spikes.

Junco, also known as crown of thorns, goes through several pulse blooms during the spring and summer months. But only its first bloom smells of rotting flesh. Thereafter, the flower's odor grows less intense. Its final bloom in late summer has no perceptible smell.

I learned that the first bloom in late March corresponds with the proliferation of flies seen every spring. Flies attracted to the carrion odor become pollinators. But as flies wane, following their initial population explosion, junco finds other pollinators to spread its genes. Subsequent blooms in late April and throughout May have a faintly sweet odor that attracts bees, wasps, and moths. The final pulse bloom in late summer entices minute insects; they are probably drawn to an odor, or perhaps color, indiscernible to the human nose and eyes.

It was the expectation of finding a plant like junco that made me want to climb onto the rocky table a hundred feet above my camp—that same table I'd contemplated camping on when I'd first arrived.

The smell of rotting flesh was strong that morning. Why I thought it to be some flowering plant instead of carrion, I do not remember. But all the while as I worked my way back to the rocky wash and ascended the mountain via the same route I had taken a few days before, I kept searching the plants to see if I could spot one harried with flies. Using a stick to push pinolío-bearing shrubs aside, I stepped slowly, no longer willing to take chances. In my left hand I held the shotgun loaded with double-ought buck, and I had two flares in my jeans pocket and more buckshot rounds housed in the baggy pockets of my khaki shirt. The night before I had awakened several times—strange noises drawing me up from my bed inside the tent. Each time I'd peeked through the mosquito-netted door, shotgun in hand, my ears tuned to any sound void of the intonations of leaves against leaves and water against sand.

There had been dreams as well: A long knife piercing the tent's thin fabric. Hands dragging me onto the sand.

Donde está el dinero?

I have no money.

Mira! Tiene una escopeta.

No, wait, please.

Mátalo!

But the day dawned windless, the sounds of thunder far to the east barely vaulting the cerro that shadowed my camp for the early part of the morning. I looked to see if there were any tracks on the sand outside my tent. But all was as it had been. I was alone, and that was good.

While eating breakfast—oatmeal, melba toast, peanut butter, sliced peaches, coffee—I watched a cayenne kite, its jet black wings in sharp contrast to its cotton white belly and chest, working its way in leisured glides and quick-tempoed wing thrusts along the river's edge. It flew directly over my camp, then perched at the very top of a tree that stood near the base of the cerro to the east. I watched it for several minutes through my binoculars. Twice it called into the forest, a subdued *meow*, not unlike that of a cat.

I could build a house within that same tree, I thought. Ten feet by twelve feet and twenty feet off the ground. It would be hard to spot even from the sandy bank. I could fish. Grow a small garden. Maybe hunt a deer if I hankered for red meat. Always in loose-fitting jeans, khaki shirts, cotton hat, good boots, and maybe sometimes a light jacket. At the base of my tree house, in a sand pit ringed by rocks, a couple of Dutch ovens. Back upstairs two good machetes. A sharp knife. Some rope. Plate, spoon, fork. A sturdy metal cup. A pillow and sleeping bag. An axe and shovel. A set of my favorite books. Some journals to write in. A dependable rifle. *Just say good-bye to life beyond the cerros . . .*

After the kite flew off I checked the calendar I'd taped to the inside cover of my journal to make sure this was, in fact, the eleventh day of my trip, the ninth day at the mountain. Back at home, eleven days flash like a sandstorm against a colorless sky. Weekends come, I'm in the woods. But for too much of my life that spell in between weekends has been something I can describe only as the Nonsense World. It is a world within buildings divided into cubicles within which we often hang calendars with pictures of forests and deserts and mountains. A place where we bring potted plants so that they too can be miserable under fluorescent lights. But at my river camp eleven days swept before me as if I were riding a bird skimming the trees and water, seeing all as it is, as it should be, as it was meant to be.

When I stepped out of the melon rock wash, still looking for a plant covered with flies, I entered a game trail entwined within shrubs and small trees, all of them planted vulnerably on limestone benches that inched out of the mountain like stacks of finely cut ivory dominoes. The trail broke into two. One led upward, the flat limestone boulders stepping randomly within it covered by the faint tarnish of minerals carried downward from the old widow's eyes, hollow and sad and transfixed on the north; as if those eyes had turned to look away from some baneful event, an act so loathsome that they could no longer bear witness to it. And yet I sensed that La Viuda knew all too well that evil cannot be spurned simply by looking away. Each day the loggers drew closer, their approach echoed by the crashing of trees falling one by one. I chose not to contemplate the widow's face for more than a minute. To do so might reveal something more infinite than what I was prepared to know alone.

So I turned and followed the other trail, under clear skies, still searching for the carrion-mimicking plant, and on a path that continued onto the table, now but a few hundred feet away. Sniffing the wind, I searched to catch again that putrid smell, and paused to check my pants legs for pinolíos. I walked on, the shotgun held loosely in my left hand, binoculars dangling from a lanyard around my neck, a canteen over my right shoulder, my cotton hat riding atop a sweaty, blue bandana wrapped thickly around my head.

When I finally reached the table, I saw that it was actually somewhat wider than I had expected. Near its center it was about forty yards from ledge to mountain slope, and its length measured at least one hundred yards. On its eastern end it was sparsely vegetated, the flat limestone exposed and bleached, with just a few small woody shrubs, like hairy outgrowths endowing tinges of green and brown to an otherwise utter whiteness.

I had at last found the source of the carrion smell. Not more than ten yards away, on a slab of limestone carpeted with yellow lichen, lay a dead deer. Its belly fat, not from adipose tissues unseen but from gurgling gases trapped inside leathers made taut and hard. I walked up on the doe and inspected it. There were no cuts or abrasions on its skin. It looked as if the animal had simply collapsed and died. I circled the carcass by several feet searching for a sign of what had killed it. But there was nothing. So I returned to the animal and took another look, the answer at last becoming apparent. Its left hind leg was swollen massively. I had not noticed this at first because the beast was lying on its left side.

Using a long stick, I turned the deer over, the black tumorous mass where it had been bitten now clearly visible. *A rattler? A fer-de-lance?* There was no way to know for sure. But it had been big and potent.

No doubt the deer had reached the table on the same winding game path I had just used. I consoled myself in the belief that this had probably happened at night, when the doe could not see the large snake crossing in front of it or coiled off to one side. But black lightning has no less force than does the white shaft splintering a stormy sky. To know either is to die quickly.

I walked on, cradling the shotgun across my chest. At the western edge of the table the monte grew emphatic and vivid. There were trees growing upwards of forty feet. A cloverlike herbaceous shrub, no more than four inches high, covered most of the ground. At first I hesitated, not wanting to venture into places hidden by such rich plant life. But it was as if some transcendental force pulled me deeper into the woods.

Stepping onto the plush green clover rug, I entered another trail, this one enveloped with vines and heavily leafed saplings and taller trees above. An enticingly cool breeze seeped past me. The sun fading as I walked farther into this wooded tunnel, corkscrew vines and small velvety-leaved trees forming an arch to walk under. The quiet growing more intense.

At the end of the trail, which must have been at the western edge of the table—though I could not know for sure because the plants presented themselves in dimensions that forbade this knowledge—I found a sphere the size of a small room made entirely of vines and saplings, and yet as densely walled as the jacales I had visited during the two days before.

There was but one way to enter this green igloo; the cloverlike herbs on the ground ushered me into a two-foot-wide opening at the sphere's base.

I stooped and looked inside, finding it hard to believe that such a structure could have been formed by accident. It seemed strangely as if some intelligence had made it, carefully folding and binding the vines and small trees so that they met in near perfect union, each growing into the others as if to become one.

I laid my hat and the shotgun and backpack on the ground and stooped forward and entered the sphere. When I sat down I felt the moisture of the cloverlike herbs against my jeans and hands. And cooler air was now falling from above, a current emanating perhaps from some hidden cave or shaft, its origins concealed deep within the mountain. A piercing quiet surrounded me. And the colors of the leaves from both the herbs on the floor and the shrubs and saplings within the walls of the sphere seemed to produce their own light—a soft yellow green.

I noticed, too, that it was impossible to tell where I was from inside this cover of vines, leaves, and branches. I could not see the mountain rising directly above me. I could not see the river but a couple of hundred feet below. I could not even see the trail I had just walked. This place was its own world. But unlike the Nonsense World, this world was lucid and unblurred by avaricious intentions.

"This *is*," I whispered.

I think about all the places I've been in my life, and how any *place* was less of a place, for me, if it was not in nature. I recall one summer when as a young man I spent a few weeks with a friend of mine in Brooklyn. Every weekend I'd insist we seek some place far away from the city, a place not overrun with people, a place with lots of trees and perhaps a lake or a stream. After a while my friend, Vic, began joking about my passion for nature.

"Just wait," he'd say. "In twenty-five years I'll go out looking for you and someone will say, 'Oh, he's living in a cabin in the woods.'"

At the time, because of whatever illogical sensitivities can beset a young man, I was not pleased with Vic's assertion that I was nothing more than a woodsman. But now, after all these years, I see that Vic was right; and I am not the least bit offended by such allegations.

But being a woodsman has not been easy. I have seen, as I've chronicled elsewhere, the destruction of so many places that were important to me. And I've grown weary of how some people have attempted to construe nature. For me nature is a place without the decisions, judgments, and decrees of humans. This is not to say that we do not have a place in nature, but that we have no right in deciding how to formulate it. Nature, quite simply, *is*. We can only know nature, therefore, when we resolve that it should not be conquered or managed or tamed. After all, a place where every living creature, whether animal or plant, has been marked, cataloged, tagged, collared, weighed, and injected can no longer be thought of as *nature*. "The wild beasts of the forests, radio-collared and drained of their secrets, are little more than unruly livestock on long leashes," says Neil Evernden. (151) If nature then is to survive, it must exist outside the objective confines of *all* humans, so that it may be allowed to remain within the subjective experience of life. If our technologies have a detrimental countenance, perhaps it is that visage that has denied us the experience of nature and instead enhanced the objectification of the natural world. But does not the prequel to such chronicles rest firmly in narratives of mind?

When I emerged from the sphere (for that is how I saw it), it appeared as if I had not entered at all. I could not see my impression on the cloverlike plants, but perhaps that was only an optical illusion. But then does that really matter?

I gathered my things and in a few minutes I reemerged from the green wooded tunnel and onto the bare rocky area of the table. As I walked, I looked occasionally up at the mountain's summit. Strangely, what had in the beginning looked so far away now seemed close, though not in a physical sense, for the trees at the very top remained small. But in a spiritual and emotional way the mountain and I had come together; even the peak that I had never walked upon was here while I was there— all at the same time.

I passed the dead doe. A swarm of flies buzzed around it. The day's heat had bloated its body to the point that a tear had formed along the outer edge of its abdomen. Above me circled three vultures.

When I reached the melon rock wash I drank the last water from my canteen. Then once more I gazed up at the mountain's summit, the place I never reached. Those ambitions seemed unimportant now. For must I touch everything to know it? I think not.

It was early afternoon when I reached my camp. I was sweaty from the climb. I lamented that the cooler air filtering into the sphere had not the strength to make it all the way down to my tent. Yet, as the bird might fly, the sphere was not more than a few hundred feet from where I now stood. I contemplated what it might be like to spend the night in it, but the time for that had passed. Tomorrow I would have to leave.

That afternoon, I packed into the canoe everything that was not needed for the night and the following morning.

I had given my knife and my machete away, and though it felt good to give my new friends gifts, I could have used both blades that afternoon. The pieces of parachute cord that had held the boxes down on the canoe's canvas and wood platform had been given to Jorge and Ricardo when they first arrived. They had asked for these to be used for fishing. It seemed like a good thing to do at the time.

Now I needed to cut more pieces of cord from a small roll I had in my pack. I thought I would have trouble without a knife, until I remembered that the cord was made from nylon. A piece of burning wood not only severed the cord but melted the ends in one quick operation.

Finally, everything was in the canoe and ready to go, save for the tent, my sleeping bag, the aluminum chair, a can of vegetable soup, some little boxes of raisins, the two water-filled canteens, the extra jug of water, the fishing pole, the shotgun, my journal. And my guitar.

I made a small fire and then decided to fish. At first nothing hit the lure, but after a few minutes I caught a bass, five pounds I guess. Cleaned it, cooked it, ate it. All was well. I did not want to leave. But I wanted to see my family. *Wishing they were here with me living in our tree house . . .*

Slowly, the sun began to disappear. I think a different sun sets there than in other places. In fact I think there are many suns, all of them shining and setting on different parts of the world.

Rain to the west and north had cleared the air. And showers lingered to the northwest—the sun turning the clouds a fiery carmine red before slipping beyond the horizon.

I had intended to write in my journal, but to do so would have taken me away from this place. Instead, I sat and listened and watched as the last fleeting minutes of daylight ebbed into the blue stillness of night.

I stoked the fire, but just enough to keep a warm effervescent glow at my feet. For a long time I sat without moving, my eyes barely opened.

And then from nowhere the old sadness, that feeling of emptiness—though not for places but instead for people and times long gone—washed quickly into me. When the reality of life's brevity and of the briefness of friendships and of love, and of the time spent with all those people who mattered and were cherished, when that knowledge strikes impudently that the times have passed and now all that remains are but glimpses that arc into consciousness like distant rainbows: you reach to grab them but they cannot be touched. And suddenly you feel you are at the very edge; the awareness is *too* real, the now *too* vivid, and you want to run and hide. But there is no place to go.

I walked to my tent and took out my guitar. In the heavens, bits of scattered light had turned a tuft of clouds bluish green. The clouds had taken the shape of a swirl, as if a painter had begun to make a question mark but had only formed the top arch. I pretended, or perhaps I should say I felt, that those bluish green clouds were my grandparents and uncles and aunts and all those I loved dearly who are now gone. There they were—looking down on me. As if to say "it's all right," and "don't be afraid." But their visit was fleeting, and I began to strum my guitar and sing to them before they left, and to the monte around me, and to the mountain who watched my torment. One last song written many years ago. I was a young man then.

> *I'll sing you a song and hope it finds you*
> *It reminds you*
> *maybe of me*
> *I'll sing it as soft as you would hold me*
> *When you told me*
> *I love you*
>
> *Maybe some day I'll hold you once again*
> *And you will know, I was your friend*
>
> *I open the door and hope to see you*
> *Just to be near you*

Once again
I'll hold you as tight as I would hold you
Have I ever told you
I love you

And you and I will sit down all alone
I'll pull you so close, you will be home

The Twelfth Day

Some people look at the earth as a work of art. Others see it as no more than a table from which to feed. Reality, I suggest, lies in both places at the same time, and in between as well. For nature does, in fact, reveal the quintessence of artistic expression. And furthermore there is nothing wrong with eating from a table that was set as much for us as for any other living creature. It is important to remember, however, that though the earth will allow endless consumption, it is not endlessly consumable. Likewise, to treat the world as nothing more than an aesthetic object is to experience only part of what nature has to offer.

Theories abound on why we behave toward the earth the way we do. Most theories ascribe our actions to historical events or philosophies and myths that have emerged from within our cultures. But at least one theory places the etiology of our actions within innate characteristics that, though not unique to the human species, are nonetheless shared by it. The theory of behavioral paedomorphosis stems from the biological observation that some species exhibit an arrestment of maturation, and therefore remain permanently morphologically juvenile. This condition of suspended development and fixed juvenile characteristics is known as paedomorphosis, or neotony in the case of species that reproduce while remaining in juvenile states.

Theorists have speculated that if physical development can be halted at the juvenile level, then behavioral development can also become fixed or entrenched at a more youthful stage: a time of directionless and often purposeless curiosity; a desire for immediate and frequently selfish gratification; and a feeling of being out of touch with the world.

Again, I turn to the work of Neil Evernden, who describes human paedomorphic behavior as "indeterminate, always in motion, ambivalent, obsessed with the 'how' of the world, and uncommitted to an environmental context." (117)

A chronological adult with the mind of a teenager. Someone who considers all things as nothing more than toys, who becomes distraught when unable to sate his or her whims, and who always wants and wants and wants.

In an article titled "Nature and Madness," human ecologist Paul Shepard agrees that at least part of the basis for humankind's behavior toward the earth lies rooted in states of mind that themselves spring from connate elements:

> In time, even with the attention of the media and a windfall of synthesizers, popularizers, gurus of ecophilosophy, and other champions of ecology, and in spite of some new laws and indications that environmentalism is taking its place as a new turtle on the political log, nothing much has changed.... [Either] our species is intent on suicide; or there is something we overlooked. (22)

Shepard adds that "a kind of madness" has beset humankind with respect to its treatment of nature.

> Something uncanny seems to block the corrective will, not simply private cupidity or political inertia. Could it be an inadequate philosophy or value system? The idea that the destruction of whales is the logical outcome of Francis Bacon's dictum that nature should serve "man" and René Descartes's insistence that animals feel no pain since they have no souls, seems too easy and too academic. The meticulous analysis of these philosophies and the discovery that they articulate an ethos beg the question. Similarly, technology does not simply act out scientific theory, or daily life flesh out ideas of progress, biblical dogma, or Renaissance humanism. The history of ideas is not enough to explain human behavior. (23)

Shepard concedes that at least at some point in humankind's past, there must have existed harmony with nature: a world where small, leisured groups foraged and were immersed in natural surroundings—a place that served as a template for both psychological and physical adaptation.

The night before I left my river camp I smelled smoke in the air. I wondered if the fires from the logging operation were burning anew.

But on that last morning I watched a storm gathering its clouds to the west and south and I did not smell any smoke.

All my equipment was packed in the canoe, the camp now thoroughly cleaned. Things were as they had been, save for boot tracks on the sand and the flattened area where the tent had stood.

The day before, prior to loading the canoe, I had lengthened its tether, then pushed the craft off the sandy bank and into the water. Once packed, the boat would have been much more difficult to shove into the river. Now the canoe floated aimlessly but a few feet beyond the shore.

I walked to the water's edge and looked northward, the escarpment where Juan waited but a distant line. I turned and gazed up at the mountain. But she had nothing more to tell me. I reached into my pants pocket, pulled out a signal flare, then held it in my left hand. The shotgun already held one flare in its chamber. I turned again and looked at the approaching storm. The black clouds to the south and to the west would provide an effective backdrop to a bright red flare, just in case anyone happened to be watching from the escarpment with binoculars or telescope. Perhaps the flare might even be seen with the naked eye. I had no way of knowing for sure, but I had nothing to lose. If Juan knew I was returning, he would set out in his jon boat. I was ready to go home.

I held the gun high and fired. The flare rose to about three hundred feet then rainbowed back to earth, the brilliant red bulb vanishing into a white smoky stream a third of the way down.

I waited about five minutes, then fired the second flare, the blast, like the previous one, echoing back from the cerros to the east and northwest and from the mountain behind me. Then I walked back to the tree line and untied the rope from the brawny trunk to which it was fastened. Slowly, I coiled the rope in my hands, gently coaxing the canoe toward me. When the boat was still in about ten inches of water, I stepped into it and began maneuvering the craft into the open channel.

This is not going to be easy, I thought. The first trip had been with the current. Now I worked against it, the storm approaching the mountain's southern face and but a few kilometers west of the cerros to my left.

A steady breeze from the Gulf of Mexico held firm at my back. So I decided that once I was pointed firmly northward, I would try out a simple invention Juan had devised and left in the canoe. Still, I dared not face the river head on. I moved instead as far to the western bank as

I could without running the risk of brushing the dead tree limbs poking out of the water like rows of caltrops waiting to rip the flesh from boat and passenger alike, if but given the chance.

First I had to cross the river, digging the paddle into a current much stronger than I had anticipated. The canoe moved ten yards sideways for every five of forward progress.

Thunder rolled over the land, and I looked quickly behind me. Tar black clouds had welled into ghouls crawling on hands and knees, their heads held out rigidly as if trying to catch a scent.

Thunder pealed over the cerros again. I was three quarters of the way across the river and twice that distance downstream from my camp. There was nothing to do but turn the canoe now, to the north, before the current swept me around the bend and I lost the advantage of the wind on my back.

I jammed the paddle into the water and held it forcefully against the current until the boat, like an old sloth, pointed its nose northward. Then quickly, I reached forward and fastened the homemade umbrella sail onto the one-inch galvanized pipe that was clamped into a turret, which in turn was screwed into the rear crossbeam of the starboard pontoon. I untied the yellow nylon cord holding the umbrella sail collapsed and horizontal to the water, then pushed an aluminum half-inch pipe like a plunger until the umbrella opened. Without pausing, I rotated my sail—two yards square of bright orange industrial-grade vinyl—until it caught the wind. Then I locked the galvanized pipe in place. Instantly, I felt the boat surge forward.

Had I not found the tree line at the edge of the sandy beach, I could have used the umbrella sail to provide a compact shade. But since I had the trees, Juan's brainchild had stayed in the canoe. The invention was sound. It could do double duty and seemed sturdy enough to withstand a relatively strong breeze. Its only drawback was that now I could not see where I was going.

À la the Spirit of Saint Louis, I navigated the river by looking left and right, keeping to the left as much as possible. Not only did the right bank have its share of caltrops, but the current moved much faster on that side. The right side was less merciful: it might slam me hard against the bank if I tried to run against it.

Forty-five minutes later the storm had not progressed any farther than the southern side of the mountain and to the west by about five or six kilometers. Or maybe it had just slowed down. It was hard to tell from my lookout.

The southeasterly breeze had not relented. Now and then I had to fine-tune the sail in order to make the most of the wind. Other than that, I rowed only occasionally and used the paddle mainly as a rudder.

Perhaps, I mused, I will write about this place someday. It will be a story about a mountain and a man's attempt to climb it. The man fails, but in the process he learns that sometimes there is more to be gained by not overcoming every obstacle.

The man cares greatly for nature. And he is perplexed when he sees it being destroyed. He has been thinking a lot about what he can do to stop the logging south of the mountain. The man is not a scientist, and maybe—if we compare him to others who have laid claim to the title—not even a naturalist. He simply roams the woods. He plays his guitar and writes music now and then. He enjoys as much the music of words when scored well on paper. Though he would never call himself an artist, he reveres greatly the art of nature.

He does not abhor science as some do. He sees and appreciates the many goods that science has brought. Science, after all, is just a method. But he also realizes that science's strict reliance on data paired with its obsession to alienate itself from emotions makes its disciples foreigners in a world so desperately in need of subjective understanding—especially when it comes to nature.

Through his journey, the man discerns that if there is an answer to saving nature then it will *not* come from science, nor from fields like economics or politics. Economics places the market at its center. It believes that the world is run by humans who are themselves run by greed. And though the behavioral paedomorphic model might suggest that, there is another side of our humanness, our cultural side, which we must call upon to curb the avarice of the juvenile—though *not* by casting out our subjective fiber. Moreover, a philosophy like economics that worships the power of money has only at its periphery any interests in the importance of nature, and then only as a means to profit from it. Politics, likewise, places the law, most of the time, at its center. But the law is the product of human special interests—too often a sententious maxim laden with autodiocentric glib.

In the end he realizes, as others have suggested, that if changes are going to occur then they will spring forth from the arts: those fields that nurture emotions, that applaud the subjectivity of relationships, that do not attempt to quantify life, that foster and cherish a state of profound reverence. Our searches and discoveries, and our yearnings as well, must be tempered with the understanding that the knowledge we gain comes to us as a gift from nature and not as some tax levied against it.

It will not be easy. It may never come about. But we must try—if not for ourselves or for our children, then for all the other life that has been forced to exist on this earth with us.

A gunshot rolled over the water. Startled, I looked left and then right. But I could see no one. Another shot broke the silence. This time I realized the sound had come from in front of me.

I flipped my paddle rudder to the left, thus turning the boat to starboard. In the distance, like the fin of a silver fish cutting a thin wake atop green water, I spotted the jon boat. I waved, but the boat was still too far away for anyone on it to see my signal.

I turned and looked back at the mountain. The slow-moving storm was at that moment beginning to surge over its summit. For an instant I had the crazy thought of throwing the umbrella sail into the water and making my way as fast as I could back to the sandy beach. I turned the paddle back once more to the left and caught another glimpse of the jon boat, now but a few hundred meters away.

Again, I glanced at the mountain, now only partially visible behind plummeting clouds. *The sphere?* I wondered. What would it be like to be inside it right now? Could it really have been as beautiful as I remembered it? Or was I merely of a mind that made it into what it became to me?

Once more, I turned the paddle to the left. As the canoe moved slowly toward the northeast, I saw the jon boat now less than a hundred meters away.

"Hola, hermano," Juan said, as he brought the jon boat carefully alongside the canoe. "How did it go?"

"It was wonderful," was all I could say.

"Don Miguel spotted your flares."

"The old man?"

"Yes. Would you believe it? I've turned him into an amateur cosmologist."

"Was he at the telescope?"

"Yes. The little one. We've been watching La Viuda for two days. But I figured you'd stay as long as possible. Anyway, there's been too much moon for any decent galaxy work. I put the big reflector scope away. We've just been using the little refractor scope."

I tossed the rope to Juan.

"I'll tie it here," he said, looping it around a brass ring on the jon boat's port side, about a foot from the motor. He pointed at the outboard engine. "We don't want to get the rope caught in the blade."

I was in the process of collapsing the umbrella sail.

"Well, did my invention come in handy?" Juan asked.

"Didn't have to use it on the beach because of the big trees. But it sure came in handy today."

"El viejito just happened to be watching the mountain when you fired the flares." Juan paused and shook his head. "Jeez, I think he's going to want me to leave that little scope with him."

"I guess it was my lucky day," I said.

"Yeah, especially with that storm coming behind you."

For a moment I had forgotten about the mountain. Immediately, I looked back to see it. It was now almost completely hidden behind a wall of black and gray clouds.

"We'd better get going," Juan said.

I stepped into the jon boat and Juan gunned the motor.

Slowly, we began to circle. The tethered canoe, like a faithful dog, followed its master.

"Did you find the Earth People?" Juan asked, grinning.

"Yes, I did."

"*What?*" A sudden look of surprise.

"You are an earth people. And I am an earth people. And so is everyone else, if only they want to be."

"Ah, but of course." Juan laughed. "That sounds reasonable."

"Tell me what you saw?" I asked.

Juan smiled broadly as he waved a hand at the sky. "I saw the very edge of the universe." He hesitated. "So what did you see?"

At that moment I turned to look back at the mountain, and I thought about the sphere. But the mountain was gone. There were only dark clouds behind me.

"Well," I said, smiling. "You saw the edge of the universe. But I, my friend, glimpsed its very center."

The Months That Followed...

Logging of the forest's hardwoods continued south of the mountain called La Viuda. The reports I had been given were accurate: a man from a nearby town obtained a falsified document stating that he was the owner of part of the land, even though the true owners were in possession of titles and documents showing otherwise.

You may have guessed—and I have alluded to it throughout the telling—that I had traveled to that region many times before, though I had never camped at the base of the mountain, nor had I canoed the river. My encounter with the parrot trappers was just one of many such confrontations over the years. On my first trip to the area in the mid-1970's I heard hundreds of tinamous every day, and the parrots were thick in the sky. On that trip I ran into a group of trappers—four men who came upon me suddenly in the woods. They were friendly and when I told them (perhaps tactlessly) that what they were doing was wrong, they simply shrugged and said there was no shortage of birds and that their actions would have little impact on the land. I'm sure the people who killed off the buffalo and passenger pigeon felt the same way.

On subsequent trips to the area, I'd run into trappers in the woods and on the back roads; I'd stop to talk to them when they opened their stands on the highways or in the markets. The birds invariably are in bad shape: their feathers discolored, their legs abraded, their beaks broken or cracked. Sometimes the trappers were friendly, other times they were not. My encounter with trappers on this journey—at the squatter's settlement where don Salvador and his family lived—was not unusual or out of the ordinary. After leaving don Miguel's and doña María's ranchito, Juan and I stopped to buy sodas at a town not far away. Some trappers were selling a variety of song birds and some green parakeets in front of the little store. Juan, who lives in a nearby city and is an old friend, was chatting with the trappers, and he called me over to examine the birds. All of them looked sickly, and one of two male mangrove warblers was missing an eye. We told the men we weren't interested in buying birds. But after we drove off, Juan and I debated our decision.

"Maybe we should've bought all the birds and then let them go," Juan said.

"But that would just encourage them to go trap more," I replied.

Over the years Juan has spent a lot of time in the area fishing, and now star gazing. Like many Mexicans, he is outspoken about the way his country is being run politically and about Mexico's crime wave and its drug trade. He's quick to point out, however, that Mexico's drug smuggling problems were caused by the United States.

"If there weren't so many marijuaneros and cocaine addicts in your country, then we wouldn't have the smuggling problems here," he says.

Juan met don Miguel and doña María a few years ago when he drove up to their casita and asked if he could set his telescope up in their yard. It was a nice flat place, and there aren't many flat places in the region. The friendship grew and Juan continued visiting about four or five times a year. Don Miguel, who had been ill for about three years, passed on a few months ago. And doña María, I've been told, has gone to live with her daughter in Matamoros. Somehow, I just can't imagine the old woman living in a city.

Lest anyone think I'm suggesting that reduced bird populations are the result of nothing more than trapping, or that I'm pointing a finger at one cause and ignoring others, let me say that there are many reasons for diminished bird populations: deforestation, pesticides, power lines, high fences, tall buildings, and the automobile being but a few.

I should explain in more detail now my association with the land I visited. In 1977 my father, Rámon J. Longoria, and his compadre, don Abdiel González, purchased two tracts of land side by side along the river. I was impressed from the beginning with the beauty of the region. It was like an island, or more accurately an oasis of green at the terminus of millions of acres of deforested land in northeastern Mexico and South Texas. Because the land was so rugged, my father and don Abdiel built cabins on a neighbor's property. It was from there that I set out to explore the area. From the beginning, I encouraged my father and don Abdiel to resist the temptation to build roads and clear the forest. However, in Mexico the law says that land *must* be worked, and if not developed it can be taken away. The origin of this law dates back to the

Mexican Revolution of 1910 when most of Mexico was controlled by a handful of ruling families. After the revolution the great Mexican ranches were broken up, and the ejido system of agrarian farming was established. Philosophers, biologists and economists have argued the pros and cons of such a system. On the one hand, the small ejidos make the country's agricultural output less productive. On the other hand, ejidos (until recently) were less destructive to the land because they did not possess large farm equipment like tractors and bulldozers.

Ironically, what was in the beginning a sound political concept to do away with the large ranches and give the campesinos an opportunity to live and farm their own property has ultimately created a situation that's generally negative toward the land. People who attempt to leave land undeveloped are at the mercy of squatters and "invaders" who come in to farm and exploit resources.

Mexican politicians often view the idea of wildlife sanctuaries as a no-win situation. After all, animals and plants don't vote. But then again, this is not a problem unique to Mexico. In the United States, politicians swayed by special interest groups (with plenty of money to finance campaigns and force their private agendas) often acquiesce to development, mining, logging, and other forms of land exploitation in order to obtain that money.

So when my father and don Abdiel left their property in a natural state, it opened the door for the land to be invaded by the loggers—who, in effect, are "working" the forest.

"Humans have overrun ninety-eight percent of the earth. Can't we leave at least two percent for the animals?" my father asked.

I think he would tell you that he didn't always think that way. He and don Abdiel are both businessmen, and their lives have been spent in exploiting resources and in construction and development. I hope my dad wasn't too disappointed when he turned out a son who wasn't going to fit that mold.

"Let's at least try and find a way to save the forest from the loggers," I told him.

Yes, I knew from the beginning who the rightful owners were of some of the land. I also knew it was going to be exceedingly difficult to save it from exploitation.

When I got back to Texas, the haze that had lingered over my campsite had drifted north, and by mid-June of 1998 had reached the upper midwestern United States. Though there had been a few brief showers during my stay at La Viuda, most of Mexico, Central America, and the state of Texas were in the bleak throes of severe drought. Fires had erupted throughout Mexico and Central America and in West and Southwest Texas. I received reports that on some ranches in Southwest Texas great numbers of white-tailed deer and exotic game brought in for hunting were wiped out when they could not escape the fires because they were trapped within the high fences that enclosed the land.

I wondered at the time if the fires I'd observed around the logging operation might too have spread onto the surrounding forest.

Desperate for help, I sought out the Nature Conservancy's Northwest Mexico program director, Bob McCready, and asked him if there would be a way to create a wildlife sanctuary on the property and thus protect it from logging, trapping, and other forms of land abuse.

I had talked to my father and don Abdiel and suggested they donate their land to the Nature Conservancy. My idea was for a complete donation, with no strings attached other than a few ethical considerations about how the place was to be treated.

From my first conversation with Bob, I knew he was the kind of person who doesn't have to be told that an area is "biologically important" to think it worth saving. Even so, we both knew that dry forests are among the most endangered habitats in the world.

"I know those areas," he told me. "The country to the north and northwest and northeast is an absolute wasteland. And the area you want to protect is a transition between three ecoregions."

Two weeks later I introduced Bob to my father and don Abdiel. Bob told them that the Nature Conservancy was working with a private conservation group in Mexico called Pronatura Noreste. He said that the Conservancy was trying to help groups like Pronatura Noreste build organizational infrastructures and that the Conservancy had undertaken a plan to promote and sustain land acquisitions in various foreign countries. He added that this would be the first large scale test case in northern Mexico.

In late 1998 Bob and I, along with my father and don Abdiel, and a man named Ernesto Enkerlin, an ecologist and Ph.D. graduate from Texas A&M University who directs the work of Pronatura Noreste from its headquarters in Monterrey, Mexico, and who teaches at Monterrey's Universidad Technológico, journeyed south to visit the land of La Viuda.

My father and don Abdiel had made the following request: there would be no development or exploitation of any kind—and that included scientific exploitation. No radio collaring, no collecting of specimens, no thermodynamic experiments, no trapping or blood sampling—or anything else that would in any way disturb the animals and plants—would be allowed. Hopefully, La Viuda would become a place where a new philosophy regarding the earth could emerge, an area where the land would be guarded, but beyond that left completely alone. We hoped the acreage might remain wilderness; after all, to claim that wilderness should be managed is to foster a belief in oxymorons.

I wonder sometimes if this idea that land cannot exist without human manipulation and analyses is not just another form of autodiocentrism. Besides, where did we come to embrace the idea that science and technology shall not be barred from any corner of the earth—even our wilderness areas?

Everyone agreed, if not with a little reluctance at first. If Pronatura Noreste was able to oust the loggers, then they would establish permanent guards to stop all trapping and logging and other forms of encroachment. It would be a private sanctuary managed by private organizations and would not be open to the public.

I realize that people must have access to wilderness if an emotional bond with the land is to be created. But there should be some places (that two percent that my dad spoke of) that are off limits to people—and that includes even those who are charged with overseeing the land. Perimeter guards only, with no wandering about within.

We stayed at a motel in a small town about fifty kilometers from La Viuda that first night. Both my dad and don Abdiel are in their seventies and to expect them to sleep in a tent was, perhaps, asking too much. It had rained hard that afternoon and when we had driven to an overlook to see the land, I thought about the flash floods that were no doubt foaming down the washes and gullies throughout the cerros. Those of you who live in hill country or mountains know the dangers of staying in ravines and low areas when the rains come.

Because of the rain, the ground outside the motel and the walls and floors of our rooms swarmed with large black beetles. There were thousands of them, and when stepped on they emitted a foul odor. My dad and I were sharing a room, and we spent several minutes trying to clear out the beetles. We gave up when we found a hole in the bathroom window where more were coming in.

Before going to bed, we all gathered in the dimly lit room my dad and I occupied. It was heartening to hear the sparkle in my dad's and don Abdiel's voices as they talked about nature.

"We want to leave a place where there will still be birds and animals free to roam," don Abdiel told Bob and Ernesto.

"Yes," agreed my father. "Everything is being destroyed."

I remember my dad casting his bright green eyes at me and adding, "Arturo, you know, wrote a book about the destruction of the Brushlands."

The next morning we drove to the great river. Just before crossing to enter don Abdiel's land at a rocky ford about twelve kilometers from La Viuda, a big helicopter, painted orange and silver, appeared suddenly from between the canyons to the northeast. The helicopter's large side door was open and we could see several men, all of them holding shotguns and dressed in camouflage, sitting inside and looking down at us.

"White-wing dove hunters," Bob lamented.

The helicopter continued on following the course of the river. I recalled the airplane that had buzzed my canoe that day as I paddled towards the mountain.

"They'll find places to land—even places they don't own. Then the hunters will jump out and shoot every bird they see," Bob said. And I thought about Carlos and how he had described the hunters he had guided years before.

We continued on, walking along an old road now almost completely overgrown. I noticed that Ernesto and I were more or less competing to see who walked the lead. He had gotten ahead of me, but I caught up to him and said, "You want to experience this place without the presence of other people."

He has a deep voice and abundant reddish hair and beard and wears thick glasses. He *looks* like a biologist. But he didn't say anything. I knew it was because he was surprised I recognized so quickly what he was thinking.

"We are the same," I told him. "We want to feel the land as it is."

"That's true," Ernesto admitted.

The day was hot and humid, like the days I'd spent beneath the mountain. When we stopped for water, Bob ambled up and sat beside me. He's tall and lanky with short brown hair and a reddish goatee. Bob drank water from a canteen, as Ernesto walked up and sat, the three of us marveling at a deep gorge studded with greens and browns that rippled into distant hills and farther into a vast plain that stretched to the Gulf of Mexico.

"The thing about this place is that you feel its wildness with each step through the brush," Bob said, reverently.

"And look at the birds," Ernesto added. "And have you noticed all the butterflies? My wife loves butterflies. She'd be in heaven here."

At this writing Pronatura Noreste and the Nature Conservancy are working jointly to try to save the land surrounding the mountain called La Viuda. They have had their difficulties in persuading officials about the importance of wilderness areas. The loggers continue to invade the land. And several of Pronatura Noreste's representatives have either been shot at, or shots have been fired in the air to scare them off, when they have gone to visit the area.

Still, Ernesto and Bob are hopeful that eventually they will prevail. To some, their plans might sound grandiose: They hope to not only save the land around the mountain, La Viuda, but also to persuade the government to establish an extensive *"Zona Ecologica"* along the river's watershed. This ecological zone would be a consortium of conservation easements and privately donated lands. In the end, they would hope to establish a refuge that encompasses many thousands of acres. Big ideas, but worth every ounce of the emotional investment it takes to think them and determined work required to make it a reality.

But lets assume that it does not come to pass. We have, after all, become used to frequent failures when attempting to save the earth. Does that mean then that we should give up—you and I? I don't think so. And I don't believe that you do either.

We will go on.

We will try to save the land because it *is*.

It is the right thing to do. It is part of us and when they destroy it they are destroying us as well. It is because we believe that desecrating nature is sinful. It is because we don't have to be told that there is some ecological or other scientific need for land to be protected. It is simply because that is who we are.

When my dad and I were driving back to Texas after visiting the land with don Abdiel, Bob McCready, and Ernesto Enkerlin, my dad said, "Son, nature is your passion."

"Yup," I agreed.

So we go on—you and I. Maybe we'll get lucky and save the land around La Viuda. If not we'll start again, some other place. If nothing else, then we'll begin in our backyards. We'll put up bird feeders and bird baths and plant native plants and set out bird boxes. We'll be less concerned with manicured landscapes and more interested in obtaining the look of a forest. Then we'll set our sights on the stream bed down the road or the plot of woods on some vacant lot. We'll plant trees and talk about nature with anyone interested in listening. We'll care less and less with trying to come up with some excuse why nature should be saved. We'll just say: *We want to save it because it is.* Then we'll walk away and start doing it.

And that's what it means to be Earth People—la gente de la tierra. So let me stop now, and you can turn the page. So we can both get to work.

Arturo Longoria

Works Cited

Buchmann, Stephen L., and Gary Paul Nabhan. *Our Forgotten Pollinators.* Washington, D.C.: Island Press, 1996.
Evernden, Neil. *The Natural Alien.* 2nd ed. Toronto: University of Toronto Press, 1993.
Freyfogle, Eric T. *Justice and the Earth.* Urbana: University of Illinois Press, 1993.
Leopold, Aldo. *A Sand County Almanac.* New York: Oxford University Press, 1949.
Noble, David. *The Religion of Technology.* New York: Alfred A. Knopf, 1997.
Shepard, Paul. "Nature and Madness." In *Ecopsychology,* eds. Theodore Roszak, Mary E. Gomes, and Allen D. Kanner. San Francisco: Sierra Club Books, 1995.

Index

agrarian: ejidos, 3, 104; farmers, 7; farming, 104; farms, 3
agricultural: chemical pollution, 22
anthropocentric: definition, 36
Arctic Oil, 76
autodiocentric: application, 68; definition, 36

Bacon, Francis, 96
birds: barred antshrike, 17; belted kingfisher, 19; black vultures, 5; blue ground dove, 24; bobwhite, 77; brown jays, 23, 67; caracara, 78; cayenne kite, 87; chachalacas, 26; collared plovers, 24, 26; common ground dove, 24; cormorants, 13; crows, 7; gray-headed kite, 29; green parakeets, 102; hawks, 67; Inca dove, 24; mangrove warblers, 103; Mexican squirrel cuckoo, 23; Mexican trogon, 57; mot mot, 23, 67; mottled owl, 40; mourning dove, 24; owl, 16, 67; *palomas y alas blancas,* 55; parakeets, 67; parrots, 67, 102; red-billed pigeon, 24, 29; rufescent tinamou, 7, 40; streaked flycatcher, 17; sulfur-bellied flycatcher, 17; tinamous, 66, 102; tropical, 5; vultures, 67, 91; white-tipped dove, 24; white-winged dove, 24; yellow-headed parrots, 6, 77
black bass, 22
Brushlands: northern Mexico, 5; south Texas, 5, 15
Buchmann, Stephen L., 30

Carson, Rachel, 30
Castro, Fidel, 82
culture, 3

Davis, Irby, 82
Descartes, René, 96

Earth: treatment, 3; work of art, 95
Earth People: definition, 109; description, 11–12, 75; dwelling, 44; finding, 101; *la gente de la tierra,* 6
ecology: academic studies, 75. *See also* environment
economic: development, 7; market, 99; Mexico, 3
ejidos. *See* agrarian
Emerson, Lake & Palmer, 39
Enkerlin, Ernesto, 105–109
environment: behaviors toward land, 3; conservation biology, 75; crisis, 29; crisis and mind, 76; empirical rhetoric, 30; problems and solutions, 76; psycho-cultural predicament, 29; scholars, 36; science, 75; technology, 75; toxicology, 75; *zona ecologica,* 108
Evernden, Neil: concentration on numbers, 30; environmental crisis and mind, 76; environmental dilemma, 75; neotony, 95; objectivity, 49; paedomorphosis, 95; philosopher and biologist, 29; problems and solutions, 76; radio collars, 91

113

fences: game-proof, 78; high, 105; Zapata County, 77
Freyfogle, Eric: on Aldo Leopold and land ethic, 54; on wilderness, 45

González, Abdiel, 103–109
Gulf of Mexico, 5, 97

haze, 5, 104
Hidalgo County, 18–19
histoplasmosis, 74
Hugh of St. Victor, 37
human: behavior, 96; desecration of earth, 20
hunters: white-winged dove, 107

insecticides: chlorinated hydrocarbons, 30; organophosphates, 30

Joachim of Fiore, 37, 76
Justice and the Earth. See Freyfogle, Eric

la gente de la tierra, 6, 109. *See also* Earth People
Laguna Atascosa National Wildlife Refuge, 33
La Viuda: description, 6; widowed mountain, 7; *Zona Ecologica,* 108
Leopold, Aldo: land ethic, 53–54; obligations over self interest, 68; private landowner, 69
Lewis, C. S., 44
Livingston, John, 76
logging: charcoal, 52; clear-cut, 7, 42; La Viuda, 102
Longoria, Ramon J., 103–109

mammals: bats, 35, 39; bear, 73, 78; coati, 26, 74; cougar, 34; gray fox, 8; jaguar, 34, 70; ocelot, 33; *oso,* 73
McCready, Bob, 105–109
Mexico: black market for guns, 83; cities of, 7; economy, 3; federal police, 18; frontera, 23, 83; government, 7; revolution of 1910, 104; rivers, 16; Tamaulipas, 3, 18–19; wildlife sanctuaries, 104
Monte Tamaulipeco, 5
music, 9

Nabhan, Gary Paul, 30
narcotics: airplane, 18; cocaine, 18; DEA, 18; Hidalgo County, 18–19; marijuana, 18; Mexican federal police, 18; Rio Grande, 18–19; smuggling, 103; Tamau-lipas, 18–19; Texas border, 18; Texas narcotics, 18; Texas state narcotics agent, 19; trade, 3, 103; as transport, 18–19; United States, 18; U.S. Customs, 18
Natural Alien, The. See Evernden, Neil
nature: ecosystem management, 57; philosophies, 3
"Nature and Madness." *See* Shepard, Paul
Nature Conservancy, The, 105–108
Neotony, 95. *See also* Evernden, Neil
Noble, David: faith and good works, 37; Franciscan friar Bonaventura, 37; historian, 36; Hugh of St. Victor, 37; Joachim of Fiore, 37, 76; mechanical arts, 37; Michael Scot, 37; useful arts, 37

Our Forgotten Pollinators, 30

paedomorphosis: defined, 95; theory of behavior, 95
parrot trappers: groups of, 102; at La Viuda, 79–84
pinolíos: near river, 23, 27, 73
plants: *Acanthocereus pentagonus,* 75; barretta, 4, 9; biznaga, 75; ebony, 5, 8; herbaceous and woody, 8; junco, 86; *Koeberlinia spinosa,* 86; *la piel negra,* 6; limoncillo, 4–5; mesquite, 5–6; nopal, 5; palo blanco, 5; palo verde, 8; pitahaya, 75
political: climate, 3; mood, 3

politics, 99
population pressure, 83
Pronatura Noreste, 105–108

quality: defined as quantity, 21

radio collar, 33, 91
Religion of Technology, The, 36. *See also* Noble, David
Renaissance humanism, 96
reptiles: coral, 41; fer-de-lance, 41, 89; rattler, 41, 89; soft-shelled turtles, 14
Rio Grande: clothes smuggling, 73; on journey, 5; narcotics smuggling, 18

Sand County Almanac, A. See Leopold, Aldo
science: method, 99; and technology, 37
Scot, Michael, 37
Self-deification, 37. *See also* autodiocentric

Self-god-centered, 36. *See also* autodiocentric
Shepard, Paul, 95–96
sphere, 90, 100
subjectivity: of relationships, 100

technology: and science 37
Texas: border, 18; brushlands, 5, 8, 15; haze, 5; home, 5; hunting, 79; Lower Rio Grande Valley, 71; narcotics, 18; narcotics agent, 19; ranches, 105; South, 8, 33, 86
Texas A&M University, 105
Trinity: humans, science and technology, 37

Universidad Technológico, 105

writer's curse, 8

Zapata County, 77